Matej Mináč

NICHOLAS WINTON'S
LOTTERY OF LIFE

Translated from Czech and Expanded
by Peter A. Rafaeli

Published by

AMERICAN FRIENDS OF THE CZECH REPUBLIC

2007
1st Edition

© Matej Mináč, Marie Formáčková, W.I.P. s.r.o.,
Trigon Production s.r.o.
© 2007 published by American Friends of the Czech Republic
© Translated, adapted and expanded by Peter A. Rafaeli
© Edited by Dr. Curtis Keim, Vera Gissing, Jessica Percha,
Tom Schrecker
© Introduction by Tom Schrecker
© Photography by Zuzana Mináčová, Tonda Daňhel,
Peter Zubal, Archives of Sir Nicholas Winton,
Matej Mináč, W.I.P., Trigon Production, Hugo Marom,
Joe Schlesinger, Vera Gissing, Tom Schrecker,
Kurt Stern, Tom Berman, Karel Reisz, Amos Ben Ron,
Lord Alfred Dubs, Joseph Ginat, Alice Klímová,
Helen James, Chad Evans Wyatt
© Photography by E.Černíková, JoAnn Cooper, Mary Fetzko,
Daniel Nový, Embassy of the Czech Republic, Washington DC
© Cover design and graphics by Petr Miškovský
© Editing and layout (English edition) by Kristine Kotsch
and Colleen Kane
© Editing (English edition) by Jan Ciganick

ISBN 978-0-9792026-0-5

The U.S. edition of this book was made possible with the generous help of the Ministry of Foreign Affairs of the Czech Republic and the kind assistance of the Embassy of the Czech Republic in the United States of America: H.E. Petr Kolář, Ambassador Extraordinary and Plenipotentiary, Dr. Nora Jurkovičová, Counselor, and the support of

AMERICAN FRIENDS OF THE CZECH REPUBLIC

the American Friends of the Czech Republic of Washington, DC: Rev. Michael G. Rokos, President; Peter A. Rafaeli, Vice President; Robert W. Doubek, Esq., Secretary; Phillip M. Kasik, Past President; and Richard Schubert.

Moravian College of Bethlehem, PA, founded in 1742 by the Brethren of the Moravian Church, was among the first to support our drive to publish the first American edition of this book.

 We gratefully acknowledge the tremendous support we received from Patton Boggs, LLP, of Washington, DC in getting Congress and others to recognize Sir Nicholas Winton for his efforts to save 669 children by transporting them from pre-WWII Czechoslovakia to England, and thus surviving.

Our special thanks to the following partners in Patton Boggs, LLP, Washington, DC office:

Thomas Hale Boggs, Jr., Esq.

David Farber, Esq.

Jeffrey L. Turner, Esq.

May they be blessed for their untiring pro bono efforts to honor Sir Nicholas Winton.

PATTON BOGGS LLP
ATTORNEYS AT LAW

www.pattonboggs.com

October 7, 2007 - Sir Nicholas meets Jeffrey L. Turner, Esq, the "architect" of House Res. 583 and Peter A. Rafaeli, Consul General of the Czech Republic in Philadelphia and President of American Friends of the Czech Republic.

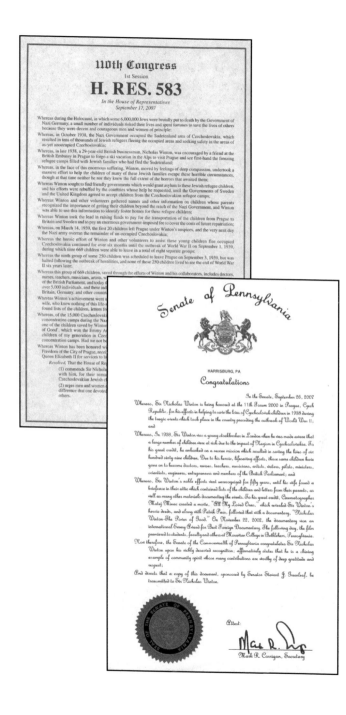

110th Congress

1st Session

H. RES. 583

In the House of Representatives
September 17, 2007

Whereas during the Holocaust, in which some 6,000,000 Jews were brutally put to death by the Government of Nazi Germany, a small number of individuals risked their lives and spent fortunes to save the lives of others because they were decent and courageous men and women of principle;

Whereas, in October 1938, the Nazi Government occupied the Sudetenland area of Czechoslovakia, which resulted in tens of thousands of Jewish refugees fleeing the occupied areas and seeking safety in the areas of as-yet unoccupied Czechoslovakia;

Whereas, in late 1938, a 29-year-old British businessman, Nicholas Winton, was encouraged by a friend at the British Embassy in Prague to forgo a ski vacation in the Alps to visit Prague and see first-hand the freezing refugee camps filled with Jewish families who had fled the Sudetenland;

Whereas, in the face of this enormous suffering, Winton, moved by feelings of deep compassion, undertook a massive effort to help the children of many of these Jewish families escape their horrible circumstances, though at that time neither he nor they knew the full extent of the horrors that awaited them;

Whereas Winton sought to find friendly governments which would grant asylum to these Jewish refugee children, and his efforts were rebuffed by the countries whose help he requested, until the Governments of Sweden and the United Kingdom agreed to accept children from the Czechoslovakian refugee camps;

Whereas Winton and other volunteers gathered names and other information on children whose parents recognized the importance of getting their children beyond the reach of the Nazi Government, and Winton was able to use this information to identify foster homes for these refugee children;

Whereas Winton took the lead in raising funds to pay for the transportation of the children from Prague to Britain and Sweden and to pay an enormous government-imposed toll to cover the costs of future repatriation;

Whereas, on March 14, 1939, the first 20 children left Prague under Winton's auspices, and the very next day the Nazi army overran the remainder of un-occupied Czechoslovakia;

Whereas the heroic effort of Winton and other volunteers to assist these young children flee occupied Czechoslovakia continued for over six months until the outbreak of World War II on September 1, 1939, during which time 669 children were able to leave in a total of eight separate groups;

Whereas the ninth group of some 250 children was scheduled to leave Prague on September 3, 1939, but was halted following the outbreak of hostilities, and none of these 250 children lived to see the end of World War II six years later;

Whereas this group of 669 children, saved through the efforts of Winton and his collaborators, includes doctors, nurses, teachers, musicians, artists, w[...] of the British Parliament, and today [...] over 5,000 individuals, and these ind[...] Britain, Germany, and other countri[...]

Whereas Winton's achievement went u[...] wife, who knew nothing of this life-s[...] found lists of the children, letters fr[...]

Whereas, of the 15,000 Czechoslovak[...] concentration camps during the Naz[...] one of the children saved by Winto[...] of Good', which won the Emmy A[...] children of my generation in Cze[...] concentration camps. Had we not be[...]

Whereas Winton has been honored w[...] Freedom of the City of Prague, recei[...] Queen Elizabeth II for services to h[...]

Resolved, That the House of Re[...]

(1) commends Sir Nichola[...] with him, for their rema[...] Czechoslovakian Jewish ch[...]

(2) urges men and women [...] difference that one devote[...] others.

Senate of Pennsylvania

HARRISBURG, PA

Congratulations

In the Senate, September 26, 2007

Whereas, Sir Nicholas Winton is being honored at the 11th Forum 2000 in Prague, Czech Republic, for his efforts in helping to save the lives of Czechoslovak children in 1938 during the tragic events which took place in the country preceding the outbreak of World War II; and

Whereas, In 1938, Sir Winton was a young stockbroker in London when he was made aware that a large number of children were at risk due to the impact of Nazism in Czechoslovakia. To his great credit, he embarked on a rescue mission which resulted in saving the lives of six hundred sixty-nine children. Due to his heroic, lifesaving efforts, these same children have gone on to become doctors, nurses, teachers, musicians, artists, writers, pilots, ministers, scientists, engineers, entrepreneurs and members of the British Parliament; and

Whereas, Sir Winton's noble efforts went unrecognized for fifty years, until his wife found a briefcase in their attic which contained lists of the children and letters from their parents, as well as many other materials documenting the events. To his great credit, Cinematographer Matej Minac created a movie, "All My Loved Ones," which revealed Sir Winton's heroic deeds, and along with Patrik Pass, followed that with a documentary, "Nicholas Winton-The Power of Good." On November 22, 2002, the documentary won an international Emmy Award for Best Foreign Documentary. The following day, the film premiered to students, faculty and others at Mountain College in Bethlehem, Pennsylvania.

Now therefore, the Senate of the Commonwealth of Pennsylvania congratulates Sir Nicholas Winton upon his richly deserved recognition; affirmatively states that he is a shining example of community spirit whose many contributions are worthy of deep gratitude and respect;

And directs that a copy of this document, sponsored by Senator Stewart J. Greenleaf, be transmitted to Sir Nicholas Winton.

Attest:

Mark R. Corrigan, Secretary

5

Publication of this book was made possible by the generous donation of Hadassah, The Women's Zionist Organization of America, Inc.

Our special thanks go to June Walker, National President, and Morlie Levin, National Executive Director.

Our additional thanks go to the following:

Madlyn & Leonard Abramson Center for Jewish Life,
    North Wales, PA
Anonymous contributor, NYC
Mr. Ivan A. Backer, Hartford, CT (Winton child)
Alan S. Becker, Esq., Southwest Ranches, FL
Mrs. Helen D. Beneš & family, Cambridge, MA
    and Little Rock, AR
Bryn Mawr Presbyterian Church, Bryn Mawr, PA
Mr. Edward Chlanda, NYC
The Covenant Foundation, NYC
Czech & Slovak Heritage Association of Maryland
Select members of the Czech & Slovak Heritage Association,
    Philadelphia, PA
Prof. Anne D. Dutlinger, Moravian College, Bethlehem, PA
Marion Feigl, New York, NY (Winton child)
Mrs. Olga Gabanyiova-Grilli, Poughkeepsie, NY (Winton child)
Stella Gabuzda, Bala Cynwyd, PA
Charles and Rita Gelman Educational Foundation, Ann Arbor, MI
Richard & Susan Grilli, Lutherville, MD (son of Winton child)
Rabbi Elliot Holin, Congregation "Kol Ami," Elkins Park, PA
Jacob Jurkovič, Prague and Washington, DC
Mr. Henry Kalan, HK Hotels, NYC
Phillip M. Kasik, P.E., Alexandria, VA
Keene State College Cohen Holocaust
    Education Center, Keene, NH
Mrs. Carolyn Rice Lord, Baltimore, MD
Allen M. Metzger, Esq., Philadelphia, PA
Mrs. Karen R. Moses, Philadelphia, PA
Tom and Mary Nemet, Jamaica, NY
Mr. and Mrs. Francis Nosek, Esq., Anchorage, AK
Mrs. Elizabeth Pick, Sonoma, CA (Winton child)
Ms. Doris L. Rafaeli, CPA, North Wales, PA
T.H. Peter A. Rafaeli, Hon. Consul General
    of the CR, Philadelphia, PA
Ms. Tamar Rafaeli, Timonium, MD

Mr. Paul Rausnitz, Miami, FL
Rev. Michael G. Rokos, Baltimore, MD
Ann Grilli Rosen, NYC in honor of her mother,
   Olga (daughter of Winton child)
Daniel Rosenberg, M.D., Willow Grove, PA
Dr. David & Mrs. Fay Rosenthal, Meadowbrook, PA
Prof. Jan & Mrs. Eva Roucek, Greenville, DE
H.F. Rubenstein, Esq., Broad Axe, PA
Marietta Ryba, Manhattan, KS (Winton child)
Mr. Joe Schlesinger, Toronto, Canada (Winton child)
Julie & Juraj J.L. Slavik, Washington, DC
Society for the History of Czechoslovak Jews,
   Rabbi Norman Patz, Pres.
Charles & Carol Soltis, Upper Merion, PA
H.E. Craig Roberts Stapleton, U.S. Ambassador to France,
   & Mrs. Debbie Stapleton
Dr. Vivian Alpert Thompson, Atlanta, GA
Deb and Joseph Weinberg, Owings Mills, MD
Barbara Wentling, Philadelphia, PA
Lewis & Dagmar White, Vienna, VA
   and The International Coordination Committee of Czechs
   Living Abroad, Prague, Czech Republic – Dr. Ivan Dubovicky

I dedicate this book to the 1.5 million Jewish children who were not fortunate enough to be saved by Nicholas Winton and who perished in Nazi concentration camps during the Second World War.

Matej Mináč

Jacob Jurkovič,
Our youngest supporter,
Washington, DC/Prague

CONTENTS:

A MESSAGE FROM THE CZECH AMBASSADOR TO THE U.S.

The time of war, more than any other human event, has the capacity to transform everyday people into heroes whose selfless acts of courage become legends for all time. Surpassing the call of duty, some individuals display extraordinary compassion and better humanity with real and measurable results. Their stories inspire hope and courage and remind us who we really are and who we would like to be. Sir Nicholas Winton is one such remarkable human being. He has been called the "Englishman of Wenceslas Square," but the most common epithet attached to Mr. Winton's name is "hero," although he doesn't like to be referred to as such.

When the early rumblings of World War II were first rolling across Europe, Nicholas Winton, then a young English stockbroker in London, opted to spend his vacation time in Prague, where he was struck by the number of refugee children in need of aid. His story of subsequently helping save the lives of 669 Czechoslovak Jewish and non-Jewish children over the nine months that preceded the outbreak of the war is finally being unfolded in these pages. After the war, Mr. Winton packed away the memorabilia of his heroics and returned to his normal life. The children he saved went on to flourish in countries all over the world including the United States, Australia, Israel, Britain, and farther afield. Today, their descendants number over 5,000 people. However, due to Mr. Winton's modest nature, his humanitarian acts went unheralded until late in his life when his wife came across the documents in an old suitcase in the couple's attic.

Since that discovery, Mr. Winton has received the international attention he deserves, including being knighted by Queen Elizabeth II, receiving the Czech government's highest honor—the Order of T.G. Masaryk—from former president Vaclav Havel, and the making of a documentary film, *The Power of Good*, about his life-saving efforts before World War II.

If the story of a young Englishman saving Jewish Czechoslovak children in a distant country before the outbreak of war is an unlikely one, it is also a story from which we can learn. Mr. Winton was an ordinary young man when he arrived in Prague for his holidays in 1938, but his extraordinary actions made a hero of him and survivors of many. His determination teaches us the wisdom of looking beyond obstacles and the humility of asking people to help simply because they can. With armed conflict posing challenges to peace, the world is always in need of visionaries who see past differences and recognize the common humanity in all of us. Heroes like Mr. Winton are role models for all ages. I am thankful to the producers of this book for bringing the Winton story into the light of day. It expands the parameters of our understanding of the good one human being can manifest and leaves us better for having heard it.

Petr Kolář, Ambassador
Washington, DC
May 2007

A FEW THOUGHTS FROM
THE TRANSLATOR

In August 2000, I attended the SVU World Congress held at the American University in Washington, DC. As part of the program we attended the screening of a powerful Czech film, *All My Loved Ones*, by a director, then unknown to me, named Matej Mináč. Later, I traveled to New York City to attend the screening of a documentary entitled *Nicholas Winton: The Power of Good*, also written, co-produced, and directed by Matej Mináč. It was here that I met Matej and his long-time friend and producer, Patrik Pašš. After getting to know one another, we realized that we were both natives of Bratislava, in former Czechoslovakia, and the current capital of the Slovak Republic. Matej and Patrik gave me the opportunity to show the documentary film for educational purposes in the United States.

In summer of 2002, my wife and I were visiting the "old country" when we learned that later in the year the documentary would be nominated for an International Emmy award. When I heard that Matej, Patrik, and their wives planned to attend the ceremony in New York, I decided to contact my friends at Moravian College in Bethlehem, PA. As always, they delivered. At the suggestion of Professor Anne D. Dutlinger and the Assistant to President Rokke, Mike Seidl, Dr. Ervin Rokke extended an invitation to Messrs. Mináč, Pašš, and their wives. The day after the documentary won the 2002 International Emmy Award for the best documentary program, the film was screened at Moravian College to a full house. I still cherish the kind note I received from Dr. Rokke a few days

At Moravian College, September 2002

later. I am also most grateful to Professor Anne Dutlinger and Mike Seidl for their steadfast support of my collaboration with Moravian. But this is only part of the story.

In May 2005, during one of my visits to Prague, I agreed to have dinner with Matej before my trip to Pilsen to commemorate the 60th anniversary of the liberation of Pilsen and Western Bohemia by General George Patton's U.S. armed forces. During our meeting, Matej presented me with a copy of his book, *Nicholas Winton's Lottery of Life*, the Czech edition of which is now used in high schools in connection with the Nicholas Winton Educational Program, under the auspices of the Czech Foreign Ministry. Out of the blue, Matej asked if I knew anyone who would be willing to translate the book into English for use in schools in the United States. I agreed to do the translation on the basis that I would donate any and all fees back to the Winton project at AFoCR (American Friends of the Czech Republic). I also told Matej that I would need to find someone to perform a professional edit. Again, our friends at Moravian College came to our rescue when Dr. Curtis Keim, Dean of Faculty, completed the edit free of charge. We are most grateful to Dr. Keim for his contribution to the project. We also must thank Mrs. Vera Gissing, a writer living in the U.K. and a "Winton child," for her editorial contribution. It was also a pleasure to work with Ms. Jessica Percha, who did an excellent job of merging the various edited versions, and who performed the final professional edit.

Finally, we had a translation and the edit, but we found ourselves with no funds to print the U.S. edition. My friend and colleague, Rev. Michael G. Rokos, President of AFoCR, brought to the AFoCR board the idea of getting involved in the Nicholas Winton U.S. Educational Project. With the support of the Czech Embassy and the Consulate General in New York City, we applied to the Czech Foreign

H.E. Karel Schwarzenberg, Minister of Foreign Affairs of the Czech Republic, Ambassador Kolař and Peter Rafaeli discuss the Winton Project at the Czech Embassy in Washington, DC, April 2007

Ministry for a "seed grant," which enabled us to get started. We are very grateful to Ambassador Petr Kolář; his deputy, Jaroslav Kurfürst; former Consul General in New York City, Aleš Pospíšil; and Dr. Nora Jurkovičová of the Czech Embassy for their support and guidance. We are not certain who all were involved at the Czech Foreign Ministry, but we are aware of the major role played by Dr. Zdeněk Lyčka, for which we thank him and others at the Foreign Ministry who made all this happen.

Our thanks also go to Mr. Charles Gelman and his able assistant, Ms. Tammee Fensch, of the Charles and Rita Gelman Educational Foundation in Ann Arbor for their guidance and advice on printing issues as they came up.

Finally, but foremost, my thanks go to Matej Mináč and his wife, Karin, for their friendship. Without Matej and Patrik's vision, dedication, perseverance, and creative genius, the world may not have learned that the efforts of one person can make a difference.

I am also grateful for the amount of attention the educational project has received in the Czech

Ministr zahraničních věcí České republiky

uděluje

ZÁŠTITU

mezinárodnímu vzdělávacímu projektu
„Loterie života"

Karel Schwarzenberg
Ministr zahraničních věcí ČR
V Praze dne 16. dubna 2007

Official auspices of H.E. Karel Schwarzenberg

Republic. In 2007, the Nicholas Winton Educational Project received the auspices of the Foreign Minister of the Czech Republic, H.E Karel Scharzenberg, who also invited Sir Nicholas Winton and his family on an official visit to the Czech Republic in October.

HONORING SIR NICHOLAS WINTON IN THE U.S.A.

While doing research for the translation of *Nicholas Winton's Lottery of Life*, I came across a very interesting document in Winton's scrapbook. It was a letter dated June 7, 1939 from the American Embassy in London in response to Winton's letter to the President of the United States. In his letter, Winton had asked the President to allow endangered children to immigrate to safety in the U.S. The government's reply essentially said, "The United States Government is unable, in the absence of the specific legislation, to permit immigration in excess of that provided for by existing immigration laws." Our country's dry and uncaring response upset me, and I felt ashamed to think of the hundreds and hundreds of children who could have reached safety in the U.S.

I knew suddenly that to bring a book on Winton's efforts to the U.S. was just not enough. I had to bring about an official recognition of Nicholas Winton from the highest level of the U.S. government, especially because the U.S. was now home to so many of Winton's children. I am grateful to U.S. President George W. Bush, who, thanks to the documentary film and our initiative, learned of Winton's deeds. The President wrote a personal letter to Sir Nicholas in which he thanked Winton for his actions before World War II, and commended the film and educational project. Sir Nicholas was proud to have received the letter. Thank you, Mr. President.

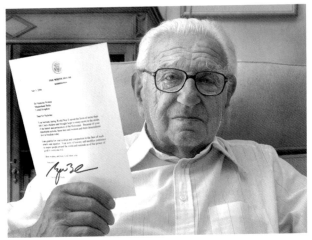

Nicky with a letter from President George W. Bush

In early summer of 2007, thanks to the support of the Czech Ambassador to the U.S., H.E. Petr Kolář, we brought the "Winton story" to the attention of The Honorable Tom Lantos, Congressman from California, and Mrs. Lantos. The Congressman, who chairs the House Foreign Relations Committee and co-chairs the Joint Human Rights Caucus, sprung immediately into action and inserted a tribute to Sir Nicholas Winton in the Congressional Record on June 22, 2007. The Chairman has also taken charge in our efforts to gain additional recognition for Nicky from Congress. The House Committee on Foreign Relations unanimously passed House Resolution 583 honoring Sir Nicholas Winton on September 17, 2007.

Congressional Record

United States of America PROCEEDINGS AND DEBATES OF THE 110th CONGRESS, FIRST SESSION

House of Representatives
The Courage to Care: A Tribute to the
Heroic Acts of Sir Nicholas Winton
HON. TOM LANTOS
OF CALIFORNIA
IN THE HOUSE OF REPRESENTATIVES
Tuesday, June 22, 2007

Madam Speaker, I rise today to recognize the remarkable and heroic acts of Sir Nicholas Winton, who personally and by his own initiative saved the lives of 669 Jewish children from Nazi-occupied Czechoslovakia and brought them across Hitler's Germany to his native Great Britain. He is an immensely compelling symbol of how the caring of one man can truly make a difference while confronting evil on a personal level. Sir Winton said it best himself in a letter he wrote in 1939,

"...There is a difference between passive goodness and active goodness. The latter is, in my opinion, the giving of one's time and energy in the alleviation of pain and suffering. It entails going out, finding and helping those who are suffering and in danger and not merely in leading an exemplary life, in a purely passive way of doing no wrong."

Nicholas Winton was guided by intuition and character. He understood the upcoming danger and realized the importance of acting fast. Having made many business trips to Germany in previous years, Winton saw Jews being arrested, harassed and beaten. Thousands of Jews fled to as-yet unoccupied Czechoslovakia, especially to Prague. Many settled into refugee camps in appalling conditions in the midst of winter. Near Prague Winton visited the freezing refugee camps. His visit deeply affected him and he felt the need for taking action.

He gathered information from parents who wanted their children out and then pleaded to countries all over the world to take them in. He also personally raised the funds to pay for the operation and continued his important struggle even though no countries except Sweden and the United Kingdom were willing to take the children in. Further, the media refused to deal with the tragedy about to unfold. The first 20 of "Winton's children" left Prague of March 14, 1939 and Hitler's troops overran all of Czechoslovakia the very next day. By the time World War II broke out on September 1, 1939, the rescue effort had transported 669 children out of the country.

I commend Nicholas Winton for his courage, compassion and foresight, for his willingness to stand up for what he believed was right in the face of indifference and to accept responsibility for being his brother's keeper. He has shown remarkable leadership, courage and ability of taking action when facing evil. Being a humble man who kept quiet about his heroic achievements for over 50 years, and without aspirations of being called a hero, he truly has shown complete selflessness and devotion to others. I also congratulate Sir Nicholas' small group of volunteers who helped him, not only for saving hundreds of lives but also for saving our faith in humanity.

As time goes by, the values for which Sir Nicholas Winton fought have increasingly penetrated the consciousness of the world. The children, grandchildren and great-grand children of those he saved will go on to establish a world where human rights and decency are the priorities of civilized society. This is the meaning of Winton's legacy to us and the meaning of our struggle for human rights around the world.

Congressional Record

We have to mention the wonderful support we have also received from the Congressman's wife, Mrs. Annette Lantos. Mrs. Lantos is a renowned human rights activist best known, perhaps, for her valiant efforts on behalf of Raoul Wallenberg, the Swedish diplomat. While in Budapest from 1944–45, Wallenberg saved thousands of Hungarian Jews. After the liberation of Budapest

23

in early 1945, Wallenberg was kidnapped by the Soviet authorities in Hungary and ultimately perished in a Soviet prison. Thank you, Mrs. Lantos, for your work in promoting such inspirational figures.

> Peter A. Rafaeli,
> Hon. Consul General
> of the Czech Republic
> Philadelphia, PA USA
> August 2007

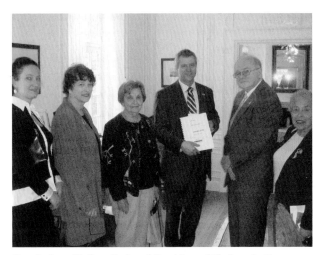

R.to L. June Walker, National President of Hadassah; Peter Rafaeli; H.E. Petr Kolář, Czech Ambassador; Alice Masters (Winton child), Morlie Levin, National Hadassah Exec. Director, Vilma Anýžová, Counselor Czech Embassy.

AUTHOR'S ACKNOWLEDGEMENTS

The American edition of this book would never have seen the light of day had it not been for Mr. Peter A. Rafaeli, Honorary Consul General of the Czech Republic in Philadelphia, Acting President of the American Friends of the Czech Republic, and a close, good friend. His optimism and willingness to help in whatever way, his devotion to achieve for Sir Nicholas Winton significant honor in the US, as well as his ability to translate, publish, and distribute this book, has made this whole project possible. Peter has produced wonderful results in his efforts to achieve renown for Nicholas Winton in the U.S., and I am deeply indebted to him. It would have been impossible for me to create the documentary film,

From left: Matej Mináč, Karin Mináčová, and Peter A. Rafaeli

Nicholas Winton: The Power of Good, had it not been for the film's editor and producer, Patrik Pašš. He collaborated with me on the lengthy research of the story and ultimate creation of the film. Together, we experienced every success and failure, every anxiety and relief.

Matej Mináč, Patrik Pašš, and Sir Nicholas Winton

Joe Schlesinger, the popular CBC reporter, donated much of his precious time and talent to the film, endowing it with such universal appeal. I cannot imagine the film without his collaboration on the script and his charismatic narration of the story.

Joe Schlesinger

Years ago, when Rita and Charles Gelman visited the Czech Republic, they saw an early version of the documentary film and absolutely loved it. They at once recognized the great potential of the story in educating young people. The Gelmans not only helped me prepare the film for international distribution, but also shared my conviction that it must be shown to the younger generation around the globe, and strove to achieve this goal.

Through their work in the Gelman Educational Foundation, aided by Tammee Fensch, Jessica Percha, and many others whom they've inspired by sharing Winton's story, the film has been shown in hundreds of schools to thousands of students across the US. Although it is amazing that a story almost 60 years old is still relative to today's children, it is even more remarkable that these children are so inspired by Winton. Many children choose to volunteer in their communities after seeing the film.

Charles and Rita Gelman with Matej Mináč and Nicholas Winton, New York, September 2002

I must also thank the Polish composer, Janusz Stoklosa – his soundtrack for the film was superb. Our cameramen, Peter Zubal and Tonda Daňhel, too, did an excellent job. Evan Lazar also helped in a significant way.

Sir Nicholas Winton and Evan Lazar

Marie Formáčková and Vera Gissing provided invaluable assistance. It was their optimism and historical expertise that helped me wade through the mountain of documents that Vera had accumulated over the years while researching Winton's rescue operation. Vera's role in the whole project has been integral from the very beginning. Without her support and encouragement, this project would never have been successful.

I am deeply indebted to Mr. Tom Schrecker, who provided fundamental support not only for the documentary film, but also for the educational

*Mr. Tom Schrecker, one of the Winton children,
with Matej Mináč*

project in Great Britain and the Czech Republic.
Today, a deep friendship binds the two of us, and I
feel fortunate that I've had the opportunity to get to
know such an interesting, wise, and generous man.

*Mr. Bessel Kok with Sir Nicholas Winton at
the Karlovy Vary Film Festival, 2002*

I greatly appreciate the assistance and support of Mr. Bessel Kok, whose confidence in the film's powerful message was a great source of strength to us. Without his enthusiasm, the project would never have gotten off the ground. Thank you, Bessel!

My deepest thanks go to JUDr. Jiří Šimáně and Mr. Jaroslav Šmejkal of Čedok travel agency and Unimex Group. At a time when the completion of the film was very much in doubt, they performed miracles. Čedok was a major supporter of the film project and helped us with travel arrangements – they even ferried Sir Nicholas Winton to various festivals where our film was being screened. The crowning, unforgettable experience for Sir Nicholas was his flight by supersonic Concorde to the film's premiere in New York City. Thank you, Čedok!

JUDr. Jiří Šimáně, Ing. Jaroslav Šmejkal and Matej Mináč, Prague 2002

I also have to give great thanks to Nicholas Winton himself and his family—especially his daughter,

Barbara, and his son, Nick—who have shown immense patience with us crazy filmmakers and have been helpful in every way possible.

*Nicholas Winton with his daughter and grandson
at the International Film Festival at Karlovy Vary,
Czech Republic in 2002*

My wife, Karin, and my son, David, were incredibly patient, encouraging, and supportive during the many years I have been working on the project. They have

*My wife, Karin, whom I call Carmen, with
Nicholas Winton in Paris, 2006*

enjoyed Nicky's great sense of humor and helped me overcome all obstacles and disappointments with laughter, wisdom, and love.

Since I have become involved with the Winton project, many of the rescued children have surfaced. Their stories are so unique and moving that the celebrated Czech screenwriter, Jiří Hubač, took them as inspiration for his new film, *English Rhapsody*. The film is based on the powerful story of a 14-year-old boy, a pianist and musical genius, who leaves his country on the last of Winton's trains to England. Although the boy finds a new life in England, he struggles to accomplish his dream of becoming a virtuoso pianist. Thanks to generous support from Czech Television, J&T, Mr. Ing. Patrik Tkáč, RWE-Transgas, and the assistance of Fedor and Monika Flašik, *English Rhapsody* will soon reach an international audience.

Nicholas Winton with one of his rescued "children," Ruth Hálová.

PREFACE

When Matej Mináč asked me to write a preface for his book about Sir Nicholas Winton and the children he saved, I was naturally flattered. However, I felt that I should decline, because there are many more famous and better qualified Winton children. But then I thought, "When will I have another opportunity like this to thank publicly Nicky Winton (as we call him today), my Scottish guardian, Jean Barbour, and Great Britain?" Between them and together with my parents and my uncle, they saved my life.

I first heard of Nicky Winton even later than most of the other "children." In about 1994 I had written to Vera Gissing to congratulate her on her moving book, *Pearls of Childhood*, and she introduced me to Nicky. Having been my savior, he now became a friend and also an occasional partner in a game of bridge. During the years that I worked for *Reader's Digest* magazine, they had a feature entitled something like "The most unforgettable character I've ever met." Nicky would certainly be right at the top of my list of such people. "Unforgettable" is, however, not really the right word. If I have to say it in one sentence, it is rather that he is one of the finest human beings that I've ever known. I am glad that I can put this sentiment in writing, because Nicky is so modest that he would probably never forgive me if I said it in public!

For a long time I've felt that perhaps not enough recognition has been given to the people who took

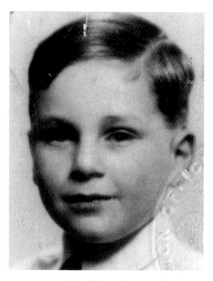

*Tom Schrecker, just before his
departure for England in 1939*

us into their homes. I think that this applies even more to the Winton children than to some of those who went on the "kindertransport" from Germany, because the Winton children were picked without being physically seen. Most of those who took a Winton child also had to pay what was at the time quite a considerable sum. I had the enormous good fortune to be brought up by Jean Barbour, who came from a very distinguished Scottish family. She was a truly remarkable person and provided me with a lifetime ethical yardstick to which I've aspired but, sadly, have never measured up. I think we should also remember that many of the people who opened their often quite humble homes to us, showed a greater foresight and understanding of the political situation than their own government did.

This brings me to my third "Thank you," which is to Great Britain. Although the British government of the time has been much criticized for its appeasement policy towards Hitler, especially during the Sudetenland crisis of 1938, Great Britain was, nevertheless, one of the few countries in the world willing to take threatened children from Czechoslovakia. It is often forgotten that, initially, the main problem for Jews who wanted to get out was not so much to leave German-controlled territories, but to obtain visas from countries who would accept them. The Nazis wanted the Jews to leave Germany, provided they left their possessions behind. It was only in mid-1941, and then at the Wannsee Conference in Berlin on January 20, 1942, that the Nazis decided on the "Final Solution," their terrible plan for the physical liquidation of all Jews. Until at least the outbreak of war in September 1939, most of the Jewish children in former Czechoslovakia and also their parents could have left if they had had somewhere to go and could pay the fare to get there. Unfortunately, most of the countries in the world had closed their doors, which makes the policy of countries such as Great Britain all the more remarkable.

Tom Schrecker and Sir Nicholas Winton
in Prague in 1999

Some years ago, Matej Mináč interviewed me for his documentary film about Nicky Winton, *The Power of Good*. Among many other questions, he asked me, "What lessons do you think the Winton story might have for today's young generation?" I still stand by my answer that Nicky Winton's actions show what can be achieved by an individual who believes in something and pursues his goal in a determined way. People today all over the world often feel powerless and think that whatever they do won't make a difference. This is not true! Winton not only saved 669 children, but also made possible all the things that these people have done for society during their lives. It is even more amazing that over 5,000 descendants of "Winton's children" are now living all over the world! The Winton story is especially powerful because, while it reminds one of all the tragedies and horrors of the Holocaust, its essential message is one of hope and optimism. It is also worth remembering that Winton was not only concerned with saving Jewish children, but any child who was in danger. Our fates often depend on luck, on chance—as the title of this book, *The Lottery of Life,* suggests. On the other hand, I believe that human beings have the ability to make a positive change in their own and other people's lives. The success of Nicky Winton's rescue mission is a clear proof of this.

Matej also asked me whether I thought that the Holocaust could happen again. Unfortunately, I believe that genocide can happen again and, indeed, we only have to look at events in Cambodia, Rwanda, and the former Yugoslavia for proof. Even more recently there has been shocking news of civil war and ethnic cleansing in Darfur (in the Sudan). Most of these places may seem very distant, but they are closer than we think – Yugoslavia is part of Europe! Education toward greater tolerance and understanding in societies can help to improve things in the future. That is why it is so important to inform each new generation about the tragedies of the past, but also the acts of courage and determination such as those of Nicky Winton. I was therefore absolutely delighted when Matej showed me some of the letters received from Czech children after seeing the documentary film about Winton. These children understood everything!

Not long ago I was able to attend some of the screenings of the Winton documentary with school children. The interest of the pupils in the Winton story and the level of their questions were quite extraordinary. I would like to dwell on just one of these questions, which was, "Were the Jews the only people threatened by the Nazis?" The fact is that the Nazis also tried to get rid of the Gypsies, homosexuals, the handicapped, and all those who opposed the Nazi party. Over one million non-Jewish Germans perished in Nazi concentration camps. Moreover, the Nazis also considered other groups of people, such as Slavs, Blacks, and Asians to be inferior races.

The vital point, which I think the schoolchildren fully recognized, is that we must all be alert to any form of discrimination, racism, and intolerance. We must try to oppose it whenever we come across it, before it grows to the scale of Hitler's Nazi dictatorship.

I am very grateful for the opportunity to be involved with a project directed primarily toward the young. Their awareness of modern history must not be taken for granted. A recent U.K. survey showed that a high proportion of young people have not even heard of the Holocaust! This is a critical time, as the last survivors and witnesses of the Holocaust are disappearing. The Winton story has been greatly strengthened because he was here in person to confirm and elucidate it. It is comforting to think that 80 years from now there will people who heard him speak about these events.

Finally, I would like to congratulate Matej Mináč

for all he has done and continues to do to tell the story of Sir Nicholas Winton's actions. I'm proud to be close enough to Matej to know the sacrifices he has made to bring his various projects about Winton to fruition.

Tom Schrecker
Sydney, Australia

When I was small,
I dreamed that I
would one day find
a great treasure.
I hoped that somewhere
in our garden
I would dig up a pot full of gold,
or that I would find
a valuable statue in our cellar;
or that I would at least win a lot
of money in the lottery...
Nothing of that kind
happened to me,
but I, nevertheless, discovered
an enormous treasure.
It wasn't gold or a statue
or even money,
It was something
far more valuable—a story
of human courage and love.

MY MOTHER'S STORY

Who am I?

At the outset, let me introduce myself. My name is
Matej Mináč, and I am a film director. I am a native
of Slovakia, but for the last ten years I have been

*In 1989 I was filming a documentary film about another
director named Juraj Jakubisko. The film was narrated
by an Italian director named Federico Fellini.*

living in Prague, the capital of the Czech Republic. I would like to tell you about the origins of one of my films, but I had better start at the beginning.

I completed my studies at the Academy of Musical Arts in Bratislava, Slovakia, and then began filming documentaries and feature films, including: *Sitting on a Branch and Enjoying Myself; One Day of a Slovak in Paris;* a five-part television series titled *The Magic of Photography;* and a few profiles about famous Czech celebrities such as four-time Olympic gold medalist Emil Zátopek, world-renowned shoemaker Tomáš Baťa, filmmaker Břetislav Pojar, and famous Czech painter Adolf Born.

Thanks to my work on documentary films
I was able to befriend Mr. Tomáš Baťa

Then came the day I found real treasure. I discovered something that in the course of just one day — in fact, in the course of a minute — changed not only my life, but also the lives of hundreds of people living on four continents.

43

I will probably disappoint you when I reveal to you that the treasure was a small book, in fact only a short passage from it, and my willingness to help my mother, a well-known photographer, who was preparing an exhibition called *Reconstruction of a Family Album.*

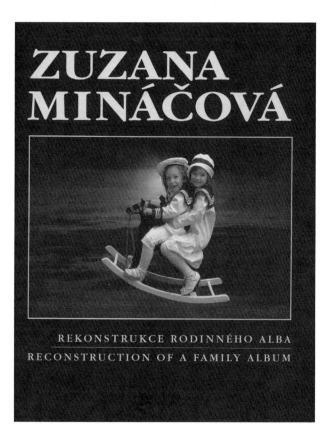

Prague
September 1996

One day, my mother, Zuzana Mináčová, made a strange decision that quite surprised me: after sixty years she wanted to recreate her childhood family photo album, because the original album was lost in the chaos of World War II.

The idea occurred to her in 1996 when we moved from Bratislava to Prague. She had reached the milestone age of 65 when, perhaps, such decisions are made!

This photograph of my mother and me was taken by Sir Nicholas Winton in 2003. He borrowed my mother's camera and took some marvellous shots.

45

My mother wanted to recreate the photos of her relatives as they were preserved in her memory. Practically all her relatives perished in the war and not a single photograph survived. It occurred to her that, as a photographer, she might be able to put such an album together again.

My mother never makes idle resolutions, so I knew that she would achieve her goal. She decided that the recreated album would pay tribute to her entire family—including uncles, aunts, and other relatives—and to their vitality and humor. Photography is an art that enables one to achieve such a task: photography can stop the clock and preserve events and the likeness of people, which would otherwise be lost forever. So, our entire family went to work on the reconstruction of my mother's childhood.

In the playground in front of our house, I found the little girl who posed as my mother in her childhood. She did not want to be photographed but, fortunately, she did want a bicycle, and so we made a deal!

*My son, David, posed as my mother's younger brother.
For the entire time we worked on the project, he didn't
have his hair cut. He was extremely unhappy about his
long hair and complained that he looked like a girl!*

I was given the role of my mother's father; my wife,
Karin, became my mother's mother in her younger
years; and our son, David, took the role of my
mother's younger brother. Our friends, all actors

47

and directors, became my mother's uncles and aunts. Mother asked us to pose for her not only because we would do so for free, but also because we closely resembled her family members. In addition to posing, I assisted in the project by setting up lights and generally as jack-of-all-trades.

Until then, my mother had never told me about her family and, quite frankly, I wasn't all that interested. Very few boys want their parents to speak about their childhood, and I had enough of my own activities to keep me busy. However, while helping my mother with her project, I heard some unbelievable stories. I was tremendously surprised by how my mother remembered every detail, and I found her stories most entertaining. My mother's uncles and aunts were quite sensational It occurred to me that the stories of my mother's relatives would make a wonderful script for a feature film, so I eagerly listened to everything she said.

Betlanovce,
Slovakia
Beginning of
the 18th century

My mother's great-great-great grandfather was a handsome man, and, apparently so strong that he could carry barrels full of beer. One day, while lugging a load of barrels, he took a shortcut through the woods and was intercepted by Jánošík and his highwaymen. They wanted to confiscate my grandfather's load, but he deftly refused to give up his beer. Jánošík was very impressed and said, "If you can lift a fifty-liter barrel of beer above your head, you can keep your entire load." My great-great-great grandfather lifted the barrel with ease, and Jánošík liked him so much that he asked him to join his band of thieves.

Famous Oscar award-winning director Jiří Menzel, who has created wonderful and inspirational films, posed as our great-great-great grandfather, a Robin Hood-type bandit. He was exceptional in his role.

Now I will tell you something that is not mentioned in any history textbook. When Jánošík was executed, his men did not distribute the loot among the poor as the story goes, but divided it among themselves! So, my ancestor became a wealthy man. Upon his return home, he purchased his entire village, including the Beltlanovce Catholic Church, as well as the Betlanovce Renaissance castle!

My grandmother was a beautiful, elegant woman. As such, my wife, Karin, was happy to play her part.

Betlanovce,
Slovakia
In the 1930s

My maternal grandmother grew up in a large family of eleven children, six boys and five girls. Their parents died at an early age, so the older siblings had to look after the younger ones, and they did so with love. All the brothers were landowners and farmers, and they wanted their lovely sisters to marry well. In this they succeeded.

My grandmother and her siblings were accustomed to a happy and somewhat luxurious life. During the summer they farmed and in winter they made up for the summer's hard work. They traveled to places where the upper crust gathered, such as Monte Carlo and Paris, and they acted as if they were royalty. They attended parties, bought fine clothes, and gambled. It often happened that they returned home in debt, but they always managed to repay.

My grandmother was different from her relatives in that she married a hard-working physician. The family ties remained strong, however, in spite of my grandfather's anger at his relatives' lavish lifestyle. Though the entire family thought he was a bore, my grandfather ended up kindly repaying some of their debts!

My mother liked to visit her relatives who lived in the Lower Tatra Mountains, where she sometimes had the most incredible experiences. For instance, she was once chauffeured around in the expensive family car by her 13-year-old cousin! There were also hunts and parties during which gypsy bands played while the family gambled in card games. During one such party, one of my mother's uncles was on a winning streak. He was so happy with his good fortune that he stuck a 500-crown note on my

mother's forehead. This was a great deal of money at the time, especially for a six-year-old girl!

This couple was recreated by the exceptional Czech actor, Jiří Bartoška, and Sabina Laurinová. Jiří liked the role of uncle Jackie so much, he ended up playing him in the movie All My Loved Ones, *of which he also became a producer.*

Mother loved her uncles a lot. They must have been remarkable men, and I regret that I never had the chance to meet them. Uncle Jackie was a renowned violin virtuoso, a charmer, an elegant dresser and a real ladies' man.

At the age of fifteen, Uncle Max took his share of the inheritance and left for America, where he purchased the famous Buffalo Bill Circus. When he returned to his native village after many years, he brought with him his American wife, Paula, a horse and buggy and also a rope, which he used to lasso children in the yard. It was great fun for everyone!

Another of my mother's uncles decided to leave for Chile, in South America. He was a real charmer and an immaculate dresser who was always seeking

I didn't have much trouble convincing the famous Slovak film director Juraj Jakubisko to pose as Maxi, as Juraj has been fascinated by circus life since his childhood.

adventure. Before he left the village, he ordered a lot of expensive clothes and left his relatives to settle the tailor's bill after his departure!

My maternal grandfather was a wise, well-respected physician, but he still had a great sense of humor. He once told my mother and her brother that a very "special" visitor would be coming and they should prepare for his arrival. He explained that the visitor was so fat that he could not pass through a double-doorway, and had to walk through it sideways. He also told them that all sinks and buckets would have to be cleaned, so they could be used to serve the visitor food and drinks. However, my mother and her brother were very disappointed when the visitor arrived; although he was quite large, he passed through the doorway normally and ate from a plate like everyone else at the table.

My mother told me of the family outings that she had enjoyed.

Once, before Christmas, my mother's father led her by the hand to the sofa and pulled out a well-hidden doll that she had wanted for a long time. He whispered to her, "You will get this doll under the Christmas tree, so forget about it for now – and don't tell your mother!"

All the family loved one another. They stuck together and made many plans for the future. They were Jews, but they didn't worry about the fact that a powerful ruler in a neighboring country hated the Jews.

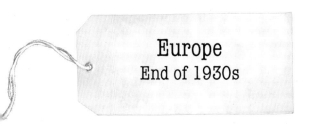

Europe
End of 1930s

The man who despised the Jews was named Adolf Hitler, and he was the leader of the NSDAP, better known as the Nazi party in Germany. In 1933, he was appointed Chancellor and began implementing the horrible plans he had described earlier in his

book, *Mein Kampf*. Although a large proportion of the population supported Hitler when he claimed that the Germans were the Master Race who would rule the world, a menacing sence of danger lingered in the air. Innocent people were arrested and often

tortured simply because they disagreed with Nazi policies. Most of all, the Nazis hated the Jews, whom they blamed for all the country's problems. They continually passed new laws and regulations that restricted and complicated the lives of Jews. The Nuremberg Laws of March 1935 took away the civil rights of all the Jews in Germany and reduced them to the level of second-class citizens.

Almost no one in my mother's family considered emigrating to the safety of another country in order to escape the Nazis. They all believed that justice and decency would ultimately prevail. After all, they had not done anything wrong, so why would anyone want to harm them? They said to themselves that, indeed, the Germans were civilized people! They hoped that all this was just a "storm in a teacup," that everything was exaggerated, and that life would soon again be calm and normal.

Unfortunately, calm was not restored, and matters got progressively worse. The Nazi leader, Adolf

Hitler, was absolutely convinced that Germany would ultimately rule the world. He hatched a plan by which all the Jews of Europe would be annihilated— and the world was soon to learn of it.

Jews were gradually forbidden to enter certain shops, restaurants, and coffee houses. More and more places hung signs saying, "ENTRY TO JEWS IS FORBIDDEN."

Jews were also required to report all their properties and possessions and, before long, were forced to hand over to the authorities all their savings, silverware, automobiles, and works of art. They were not permitted to have telephones, were subjected to strict limitations on shopping hours, were expelled from all clubs and associations, and Jewish children were prevented from attending public schools. They were not allowed to go to the movies or walk in the park. My mother still remembers how devastated she was that she could not see the movie Nine Hours of Chemistry, with the then famous actress, Alida Valli, when all the other children were raving about it.

Hitler expanded his evil empire by invading and occupying more and more land, including entire

European countries. In March 1938, Hitler's armies marched into Austria without a fight. Next was the occupation of the Sudetenland, the border region of Czechoslovakia, in September 1938. By March 15, 1939, the Germans occupied the remainder of Bohemia and Moravia.

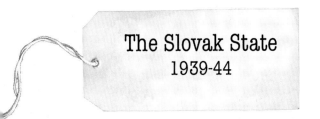

The Slovak State
1939-44

In March 1939, Slovakia declared its independence from Czechoslovakia. However, its government had no power, and its politicians were puppets with Nazi Germans pulling their strings.

The next indignity imposed on the Jews was a new law forcing them to wear a yellow star to identify

them as part of an undesirable race. In this way, they were practically prisoners in their own homes.

The Nazis began building large prisons for Jews, as well as for opponents of the Nazi regime. These jails were called "concentration camps," and most of them were in Poland, Germany, and Austria. Men, women, and even children were transported to these camps from various countries and territories, including Bohemia, Moravia, and Slovakia, the territories of the former Czechoslovakia. The inmates suffered unimaginable hardship and torment. Of those who were not immediately sent to gas chambers that were specially built for mass executions, many perished in the camps from hunger or infectious diseases.

Their only offense was that they were of Jewish origin. Six million people died in these camps! The Nazis' terrible crime was later referred to as the Holocaust.

My mother is Jewish, and for that reason her childhood ended at the age of nine, when her fight for survival began. She was hidden for some time in Bratislava, Slovakia's capital, but in September 1944, someone betrayed her hiding place. A German patrol caught her, and she was deported to one of the worst concentration camps—Auschwitz, in Poland. Miraculously, she survived, thanks to a great coincidence and a huge stroke of luck.

During the selection conducted by the notorious Dr. Mengele, who chose which prisoners lived and which died, children under the age of sixteen were supposed to step to one side and the older ones to another. My mother stepped to the side with the mothers and young children, not knowing that this group was to be sent immediately to the gas chambers. An older cousin, who was a veteran of Auschwitz, saved her. When she saw my mother, she pulled her quickly into the other group, one that was earmarked for slave labor in the German Reich.

My panic-stricken mother screamed because she was petrified, but her cousin knew what needed to be done. She slapped my mother so hard in the face that she was absolutely shocked and immediately silenced. From this moment on, my mother stopped drawing attention to herself, and she survived!

Of every thousand people deported to Auschwitz, only a handful survived. The Germans imprisoned not only Jews, but also all those whom they considered their enemies – and they had a lot of enemies!

WINTON'S STORY

Prague
December 1997

I decided to make a film about my mother's story, but I thought that the tragic fate of my amusing and happy relatives was too sad. I felt that something positive was necessary, a shining ray of hope within the dark sea of evil called the Holocaust. I searched everywhere for a happy story. In every library in Prague, I read everything I could get my hands on, but still found nothing that could redeem and complete the story of my family.

I constantly visited the library of the Jewish Museum in Prague. On one of my visits, I noticed that the staff members were not at all pleased to see me, and I was not surprised. On every visit I borrowed twenty or thirty books and always created chaos. What's

more, I frequently did not return books on time. The librarians didn't appreciate that.

However, I was not discouraged and continued to search the bookshelves. Suddenly, one book drew my hand like a magnet. I opened it, and was struck dumb when my eyes fell on one paragraph:

"We were a diverse group of children who had only one thing in common: we had all escaped from Nazi-occupied Czechoslovakia. Some children escaped with their parents, but many, like me, came alone on a children's transport. That we managed to get away was due above all to the efforts of one man—a stockbroker from London, Nicholas Winton."

The small book I held in my hands was *Pearls of Childhood,* written by Vera Gissing. In her book, she reminisces how, as an eleven-year-old girl, she went on an unexpected journey to England that saved her life. Although her parents perished in the Holocaust, an English family adopted and cared for her. Three years later, she attended the Czechoslovak school in Wales.

I will never understand how I had never noticed that book. After all, I had searched the shelf from end to end. But now I held it in my hands for the first time.

"Eureka, I've found it!" I exclaimed, like Archimedes in ancient times. I knew that I had hit my target. The book was what I needed to film the story I had in mind.

I had found the missing piece to the puzzle of my film script. I was delighted, but had not yet realized that I had discovered a golden treasure that would not only turn my own life upside down, but would also influence the lives of hundreds of people around the world.

Goosebumps and all, I immediately asked the librarians if I could borrow the book. Unfortunately, they considered me a very unreliable person and replied, "Certainly not! You can borrow it only after you return all the other books! We know you: you take half the library and disappear for months. Soon we will have nothing left to loan to others!"

I tried in vain to convince them to change their minds, but they left me no choice but to sit down and read the paragraph over and over until I could remember it by heart. As I was leaving the library, I saw the staff felt sorry for me, but by then I no longer needed the book! The paragraph was etched in my brain.

At home I sat down and started to work on the script of the film that had originated from my mother's memories. I incorporated into the script the story of the children who were saved by Nicholas Winton. I decided to make the film's hero a child who escaped to England on one of Winton's trains and survived the war.

I took the completed script to a well-known translator in Prague to have it translated into English, so I could look for co-producers and investors for the film.

As the translator began to read the script, she turned to me and said, "You know, there are some inaccuracies in your description. For instance, the children had numbered signs hanging around their necks!"

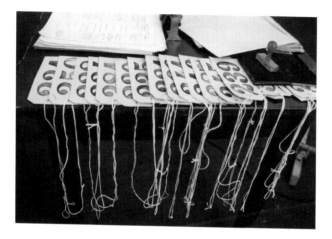

"How would you know?" I objected. "Were you there?"

"Yes," she replied, "I was."

"What?" I was taken aback. "You were at the train station that day?"

"Yes, I was one of the children."

I was stunned. One of the children? Not in my wildest dreams did I think I would ever meet one of them. While I was writing my script, I felt that I was describing a long-forgotten event in history.

"That is marvelous," I exclaimed. "I am sure that you will be able to help me with the details."

"I am not sure that I can be of any help," she said. "I was only four years old then, and I don't remember much. Why don't you try one of the other rescued children? There are about seven hundred of us in all. Or you could ask Mr. Winton himself."

I was shocked. "Mr. Winton?" I gasped. "Is he still alive?"

When one learns about a historical figure, one automatically assumes that the person is no longer alive, and that everything had happened so long ago that any evidence of it now exists only in some archive. Nonetheless, the translator gave me a note with Winton's phone number and address and said, "Of course he is still alive! He lives just outside London at a place called Maidenhead."

A portion of a letter written by Winton in 1939

A phone call to England
January 1998

Back home, with knots in my stomach, I dialed the number the translator gave me.

A gentleman with a very pleasant voice answered. I was so nervous, I asked him twice whether I was really speaking to Mr. Nicholas Winton! Once I calmed down, I explained to him that I was a film director from the Czech Republic, and that I would love to pay him a visit. I also explained to him why I wanted to see him.

"Yes indeed, certainly, young man, I will be delighted to talk to you," Winton replied. "Hold on a second, I have to check my calendar to see when we can meet. This week is booked, and so is the next one, and the one after that is even worse."

Finally, this ninety-year-old, incredibly busy gentleman and I agreed that we would meet four weeks later, between two and four o'clock.

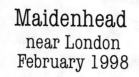

Maidenhead
near London
February 1998

Four weeks later, in Maidenhead near London, at exactly two o'clock, I pressed the doorbell of a

Nicholas Winton in his garden in 1998

neat house surrounded by a spacious garden. I was really more nervous than I had been in a long time. I felt worse than when I was taking my final school exams!

What does someone who saved nearly seven hundred children look like? What does a real hero look like? I had only come across them in films or books, but I had never before met a real hero.

Suddenly, the door opened, and a quite ordinary man stood in front of me. He certainly didn't look like he was about to celebrate his 90th birthday! We greeted each other, and I noticed a twinkle in his eyes.

We spoke at length. He was very congenial and funny, having what we call a dry English humor. It was a pleasure to be in his company while he spoke about his life, his children and grandchildren, and his love for gardening and opera. When I asked him to pose for a photograph, he quickly got down on one knee, and I was amazed by how agile he was, considering his age. He noticed my surprise and explained that he swam daily in his pool — and the pool wasn't even heated!

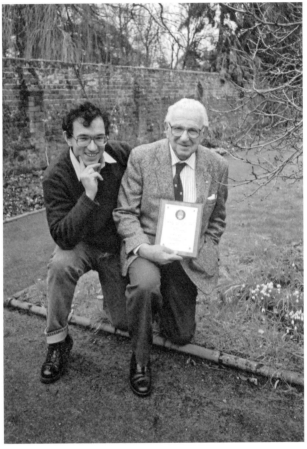

My first visit with Nicholas Winton, 1998

"I would never get into such cold water," I said, shivering after testing the pool with my hand.

"Well," he reassured me, "no one asked you to, did they?"

Already during my first visit with Nicholas Winton, I knew that I would be making more than a feature film. My director's heart was telling me that I must create a documentary film about this remarkable man.

When I asked him what had motivated him in 1939 to rescue all those children, he just waved his hand and said that anyone in his place would have done the same.

"Not everyone else would have acted as you did," I objected. "After all, you were the only one!"

He quickly responded, "Why are you making such a big deal out of it? I helped just a little, and I was at the right place at the right time."

I could not understand his attitude. Why didn't he want to talk about his rescue mission? He acted as if he thought that everything he had done was quite ordinary. But he was an experienced and intelligent individual, and he must have realized that what he accomplished was exceptional.

I was facing a dilemma that I was determined to solve, and I could hardly wait to begin working on my new film. I hoped that I would then find the answers to the following three questions:

Why did he do it?
Why was he silent for half a century?
How did he accomplish it?

But how could I get Mr. Winton to talk about what he did? Then, a very simple solution occurred to me: what if I invited him and his wife, Greta, to Prague?

Perhaps seeing familiar places in Prague would help Winton remember the days he spent there sixty years ago.

To my delight, the Wintons accepted my invitation.

Prague
March 1998

When one invites special guests to stay, it is expected that one will take good care of them. With a great deal of difficulty I scraped together enough money to pay for Mr. and Mrs. Winton's visit. Everything was planned meticulously, and I could hardly wait for them to arrive. I decided that, together, we would follow the trail of Mr. Winton's stay in Prague in 1938 and 1939. I was convinced that I would be able to extract from his memory more than one gem of specific recollection.

My first question was to ask where he would like to stay during his visit.

He responded that he would, of course, like to stay at the Hotel Šroubek in Wenceslas Square, where he lived and worked during his first visit to Prague. I scoured the Prague telephone directory, but was unable to find the Hotel Šroubek. So, I strolled at random into a hotel on Wenceslas Square and asked the staff if they had heard of it. "The hotel has been renamed," they told me. "We are now the Hotel Europa."

Nicholas Winton in the Hotel Šroubek again after 59 years

I decided to reserve a room at once, and I already knew which one I wanted. I reserved suite number 171, the very one in which Mr. Winton had lived and worked during his stay in Prague sixty years before.

The suite consisted of two rooms: one he used as an office, and the other as a bedroom. When I brought the Wintons to suite 171, Mr. Winton was very surprised! "Yes, yes, I do recognize it!" he said. "Here was a little table where I filled out all the applications, and here is where I used to sit with my friend Martin Blake, who had asked me to come to Prague in the first place.

"And this is where I received the parents. They began knocking on the door in the early morning hours, sometimes while I was still shaving. When we met, they wanted to know what opportunities there were for their children to leave the country safely.

"And in this coffee shop we had our headquarters…"

I was elated. Every chair, every piece of furniture reminded him of something. Deep down, I was grateful that almost everything in the hotel had remained in its original condition. What amazed me most was how much Mr. Winton remembered.

The Wintons in Prague

Prague
Winter 1938/39

Chance plays a significant role in human life. Even Nicholas Winton began his heroic deeds by sheer coincidence. In December 1938, he was planning a winter vacation in the mountains.

"I was twenty-nine years old. I lived in London, and I was working at the Stock Exchange. I was packing my ski equipment, preparing to go on vacation to Switzerland with my friend Martin Blake, a teacher at the Westminster School, when the phone rang. It was Martin: 'I've canceled the skiing trip, and I am calling from Prague. Forget the skis and join me immediately! I have something much more interesting than skiing for you here,' he told me."

So, shortly before Christmas 1938, Winton departed for Prague. He loved a good adventure. Moreover,

he had enough money, he liked having a good time, he was fond of girls, and generally enjoyed life; he didn't mind a change in plans.

When Winton arrived in Prague, Martin Blake immediately took him to visit several refugee camps near the city. He explained to Winton that thousands of refugees from the Sudetenland region had been forced to leave their homes at a day's notice and

The Munich Agreement, September 1938

with only the barest of necessities when England and France signed the Munich Agreement in September 1938. The agreement had given Czechoslovakia's border regions to Hitler without a fight.

The refugees from the Sudetenland were living under extremely harsh conditions. It was freezing in the snow-covered camps, there was no heating, and all suffered from a lack of food and clothing.

Martin Blake worked as a volunteer for an organization called the British Committee for Refugees, which worked to get as many adults to safety as they possibly could. But they were having great problems in doing so, as no democratic country was willing to accept so many people. This is why Blake summoned Nicholas Winton. He knew Winton well and was confident that the obstacles would never discourage him.

And he was right! Winton immediately began to look for ways to help Blake. While doing so, he was horrified to learn that no organization was helping the children at risk. Was there anything that could be done to help them? After all, every country had very restrictive immigration laws. To get the children to a safe haven would be nearly impossible.

Moreover, Winton had obtained confidential information that Hitler would soon occupy the remainder of Czechoslovakia. A clerk at the German Embassy in Prague allowed him to see a map that illustrated how Germany planned to occupy the rest of Europe! The map included specific timetables, and Winton saw that there was not much time left for Czechoslovakia. It was also clear from these secret documents that an all-out war would erupt

Deutſchland, Deutſchland über alles!

within eight months. If that were to happen, no more children could safely escape the country. Winton realized that anyone left behind would be in great peril. The cruelty with which Hitler treated Jews in Germany convinced him that he would show no mercy to Jews in Czechoslovakia.

Winton constantly asked himself, "What can be done?" He knew that he, personally, could adopt two or three children and take them to England, but that would not solve the greater problem. What he really needed was a way to save all the children at risk.

Winton knew that Great Britain had relaxed its immigration laws after the terrible Kristalnacht massacre in Germany on the night of November 9, 1938. The "night of the broken glass" was a well-planned attack against the Jews during which the Nazis burned more than 1,000 synagogues and plundered more than 7,000 Jewish businesses. Many Jews died or were imprisoned. In an effort to help, the British government agreed to admit a limited number of Jewish children from Germany and Austria. Winton wrote to inquire whether he could get permission to bring the endangered Czech children to England as well.

REPORT ON THE PROBLEM OF REFUGEE CHILDREN IN CZE(

It is not possible at the moment to g
of the number of children in Czecho-Slovakia who m
This is due to the fact that many middle-class fami
were forced to leave their homes, first of all
At that time they thought that provision would be m
within a very short time. Now, however, that four
elapsed, these friends are unable to offer hospitali
with the result that continually more and more famil
registering themselves as refugees. A conservative
number of children who can leave Czecho-Slov
These are roughly 85% Jewish and 15
largely from the middle-cl
fathers having b
solicito

Winton's 1939 request

He received a positive response, subject to some specific conditions. He would have to obtain a guarantee of 50 British pounds for each child, which,

at the time, was a considerable amount of money. Furthermore, he would have to find British families willing to commit in writing to care for these children until they were 18 years old. Winton had to raise the funds necessary to cover the children's

Winton's application form from 1939

travel expenses to England and to run offices in both Prague and London.

Most people, when faced with apparently insurmountable obstacles, would decide to give up. Indeed, Winton was an ordinary person with no special contacts, no money, and no time to spare. However, Winton would not be himself if he gave up. To him, the rescue mission became a challenging venture in which he was determined to succeed, no matter what!

His first step was to establish an organization that could assist the Czech refugee children. To his horror, he discovered that it would take months to complete the legal process to form such an organization. Winton came up with a brilliant, very original solution to avoid any bureaucratic hurdles. He had forms printed with the heading "COMMITTEE for REFUGEES from CZECHOSLOVAKIA— CHILDREN'S SECTION." He called for a meeting with himself and appointed himself Honorary Chairman of his made-up organization. He even

ordered an official rubber stamp. Now he was ready for business!

Winton made a list of several hundred threatened children whom he wanted to get to England as

quickly as possible. When he wrote to friends in England about the plight of these children, who lived in such poverty that they could not go to school and often went hungry, his friends were appalled and inspired to help. In just a few weeks' time, Winton had enough willing foster parents to begin

bombarding the British Home Office with requests for the children's entry permits.

But the British officials merely shook their heads at Winton's requests. "What's the big rush?" they reasoned. "Nothing bad will happen in Europe. Hitler will be satisfied with what he already has, and no harm will come to these children of yours. We will carefully consider your requests, but we need time to issue visas. Just be calm and wait for our decision."

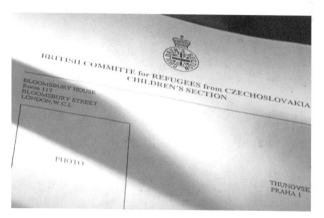

"Why didn't anyone, not even government officials, believe that danger was imminent?" I asked him later.

"It is much more convenient not to believe. Then you can just sit back and do nothing, and that suited those officials perfectly," Winton replied with a smile.

At that time, saving the children was the most important thing on Winton's mind. Nothing else mattered.

While still in Prague, he spent long hours speaking with the children's parents to convince them that

their children were in imminent danger and must be taken to safety.

The news of Winton's efforts spread quickly through Prague. Winton soon opened an office on Voršilská Street in the heart of the city. Before long, lines of anxious parents waiting to see Winton stretched for blocks and blocks.

Requests for help poured in from all corners of the Czech lands. The task was very challenging, and it seemed to Winton that 24 hours a day weren't enough. Fortunately, Trevor Chadwick, a former schoolteacher, offered to work with him. "Without dedicated and noble-minded people, which Trevor certainly was, our rescue efforts would never have succeeded. I never missed a reception or meeting and used every opportunity to find new allies," Winton recalled.

At one such event he met a beautiful Swedish woman who worked for the Red Cross. He was very pleased because he thought she might help him get some of the children to Sweden. He wanted to confide in her about his plan, but soon was warned that the beautiful Swedish lady was actually an undercover Gestapo agent! The Swedish Red Cross was just an alibi so she could get close to those who were helping refugees. Winton was told not to have further contact with her, as it could be dangerous.

This he refused to do. Besides, he already had official permission to transfer some children to Sweden. The plane had been reserved, so he saw no need to cancel anything.

Thus, already in December 1938, Winton had managed to get the first twenty children from Prague to Sweden by air, and he had done it with the full knowledge that the Gestapo was closely following his activities. Winton never worried; he was convinced that his British citizenship gave him protection.

Nicholas Winton in 1939

Prague
March 1998

"Well Nicky, you were a real James Bond! Weren't you afraid German spies might arrest you and whisk you away to Germany for interrogation?" I asked him.

Winton shrugged off my question with a smile. "Matej, you are exaggerating. It really was not all that dangerous, and as it turned out, I succeeded. We managed to get a group of children to Sweden. It was our first big success, and it gave us much encouragement. It proved to me that we could get children to safety.

"In fact, because we are now in Prague [for this interview], it would be nice if we could pay a visit to the Swedish Embassy to thank them for the help they gave us at that time."

I placed a call to the Swedish Embassy in Prague and explained what I was doing. We agreed that the "Winton children" living in the Czech Republic would meet their rescuer at the Swedish Embassy. It occurred to me that the news media might want to write about the reunion, so my colleague, Martina Štolbová, informed ČTK, the Czech Press Agency.

When we arrived on time at the Swedish Embassy, we were surprised to see a lot of activity around the main entrance. There were dozens of cars and many television crews and reporters. The building was open

and fully lit, and there was a sea of photographers and people with microphones in their hands.

"Oh, this is unpleasant," I exclaimed. "They must be holding an important event and forgot to tell us about it!" I was worried and even a bit annoyed: "We planned this well in advance! If they were expecting an important visit, we could have rescheduled our get-together for another time."

Meeting with the rescued children at the Swedish Embassy was very emotional

As we approached the large group of journalists in front of the Swedish Embassy, I was startled to see them coming toward us. It seemed that they were all waiting for us! Well, to be more precise, they were all waiting for Mr. Nicholas Winton.

While I watched this journalistic assault with much amazement, I noticed that Winton was really enjoying himself. The attention did not bother him one bit, and he kept smiling as he answered dozens of questions. I thought to myself, "Just yesterday you told me that fame is worthless!"

After a while, Winton leaned over to me and whispered, "The Swedes will never let you down. Even then they were the first ones to step up to the challenge and help us."

I was pleased. The meeting with the rescued children was very emotional and touching, which convinced me that the Winton story would appeal to people of all ages and nationalities.

Prague
Winter 1938/39

The news of the Englishman who had managed to get a group of children to safety in Sweden spread like wildfire. Suddenly, Winton's list contained 5,000 children's names. Although the bureaucrats at the British Home Office were still moving at a snail's pace in issuing entry visas, Winton was determined to remain calm. "If they need that much time to issue visas," he thought to himself, "I might as well print them myself." He found a print shop in Prague willing to print false British visas for

him. To his great surprise, the meticulous Germans never spotted the forgeries. They dutifully stamped each one of them, allowing the children to leave the country.

Meanwhile, Winton's office in London managed to obtain the real British entry visas. While the

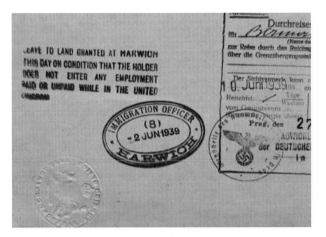

children were on their way to England, the fake visas were exchanged with the real ones. In this way, Winton gained precious time, which enabled him to send even more children to Britain. Those forged documents were absolutely perfect! Even now, after so many years, it is almost impossible to detect which of the documents are real and which are not.

In January 1939, when Winton was busiest in Prague, his boss at the London Stock Exchange contacted him and demanded that Winton return immediately to England. Apparently, the gold trade in South Africa was at its peak. Winton explained to his boss that, unfortunately, he could not leave Prague at the moment, because he had to look after Czech and Slovak children who were in danger. His boss was unimpressed.

"It is noble of you that you are concerned about children who are strangers to you. I admire that.

During the winter of 1939 Nicholas Winton met many families in Prague

But, all kidding aside, this is a serious matter. We are talking about gold here!"

"Is gold more important than children?" Winton countered. He realized that he and his boss would never see eye to eye. He did not care whether he would lose his job; that seemed irrelevant just then. He knew he'd always find work, but what he was involved in now simply could not wait!

CREWS & C?

Partners:
J.E HART   W.S BARNARD
J.A ELLIOTT   J.H.T.WORTH
J.M HOPKINSON   R.GLANVILLE
R.F.ALGER

(TELEGRAMS:)
CREWS, STOCK, LONDON.

TELEPHONE
METROPOLITAN 7381 (5 LINES)

30. *Throgmorton Street.*

London. E.C.2

9th January, 1939.

N. G. Winton, Esqre.,
Grand Hotel Stroubek,
Prague,
CZECK.

Dear Winton,

I have returned to-day to the City after a nice holiday at my new Villa in the South of France. There is very little doing in the Kaffir market; but I would sooner you were taking a rest here, rather than doing here the work for thousands of poor devils who are suffering for no fault of their own. You are more experienced than Cooke and there is always something in a small way to be done and to study. For instance, I still think Western Holdings will go lower - probably West Wits and Western Reef also. There is so much new capital required, both in South and West Africa, that there is little chance of good markets while all this fresh money has to be found.

Mr. Chamberlain's visit, we all hope, will produce some good, and if this is the case, we hope you may be able to get back to the office here by next Monday.

With best wishes for the New Year and may it be more profitable for you than last.

Yours sincerely,

Geoffrey Hart

The letter from Winton's boss, demanding that he return to London promptly and stop bothering about " thousands of poor devils."

Winton was happy to leave the Stock Exchange, and he didn't return after World War II ended. He became disgusted with that world in which money and gold meant more than human life. He could not stand people who made money their God. He knew that their God was more false than his falsified documents.

When I asked whether any documents from the time had been preserved, Winton's wife Greta told me another incredible story.

Maidenhead
near London
April 1988

In spring 1988, Greta began to clean the house as she did every year. This time around, however, she decided to do a more thorough job and get rid of all the excess junk in the attic, which had not been cleaned in years. Not wanting to throw out anything valuable, she carefully and meticulously inspected each dust-covered item, including a very old suitcase. Expecting to find in it nothing but old clothing, she was surprised to see that it contained all sorts of documents. She didn't recognize the papers, so she started to read them.

Greta was so immersed in reading these documents that she might have spent all night in the attic if it hadn't started to get dark.

Among the papers were letters and photographs. Much of the writing was in a language that she could not understand. She judged it to be a Slavic language, since many of the letters had hooks or dashes above them. When she came upon some forms of the word "Praha," she realized that these papers related to Prague and Czechoslovakia.

"What is all this?" she later asked her husband.

He simply waved her off and said, "That is such an old story. It certainly would not interest you."

On the contrary, Greta was extremely interested, and she pressed her husband to explain what she had found. She was astounded to hear what he had done so many years ago in Czechoslovakia and how many children he had saved from certain death.

"Nicky, what will we do with all these things?"

Without hesitation, he replied, "What should we do with them? We'll burn them! After all, you do want a clean attic, don't you?" She completely disagreed with him.

"We have no right to do that," Greta objected. "Take a good look at everything that is here," she said, as she placed letter after letter in front of him. The letters were written by the anxious parents of Winton's "children," suggesting how to take care of

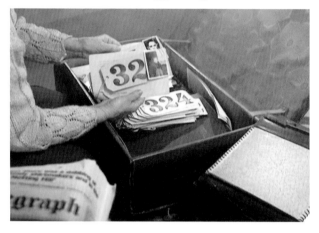

them, what they liked and disliked, what games they liked to play and what food they liked to eat.

"These parents probably did not survive, and their letters should be given to their children, who never received them," Greta decided.

The suitcase from the attic contained photographs of children who survived, but also photographs of those who were not so fortunate. It included documentation of the obstacles Nicholas Winton had to overcome, and what he had to do to rescue the children. There were telegrams, permits stamped by the German occupation authorities, and information about trains departed or delayed. Most importantly, Greta found the list of the 669 children who were rescued.

Thinking out loud, Greta mused, "I wish I knew

Nicholas Winton and his wife, 1998

what those children look like today!"

Her husband just shrugged his shoulders; he was not very enthusiastic about dusting off what was to him ancient history. He didn't want to look back. The past was of no interest to him. Instead, what interested him was what lie ahead!

"After I found the documents," Greta explained to me, "I offered them to various institutes, hoping they would keep them and maybe would offer them to the children to whom the letters and photographs belonged. No one expressed interest in the materials until we contacted the Yad Vashem Holocaust Museum in Israel, which was thrilled to accept every single item for their archives. Today, they are still carefully protected there."

Naturally, I visited Yad Vashem as soon as I could. I hoped my visit would give me a better insight into Winton's incredible deed.

Jerusalem,
Israel
May 1998

Jerusalem is a gorgeous city. Its history goes back several millennia, and being there makes one feel that historical or biblical events could occur before one's eyes. There one will find Mount Zion and the place where it is said that the Last Supper took place. East of the city is the Mount of Olives and the Gethsemane Garden in which Judas betrayed Jesus. The suburb of Ein Karem is the alleged birthplace of John the Baptist.

Of course, I didn't see any of this! I stayed at the Yad Vashem Memorial from morning until night and sat at a tiny desk in an underground room with no windows, which doubled as an air raid shelter. There was no room for me anywhere else, because other researchers occupied all the other desks, and I couldn't wait to start my work. Instead, I gratefully accepted the place I was given.

The librarians brought me a thick scrapbook that Winton's secretary, Barbara Wilson, created during World War II. Barbara voluntarily worked for him in his London office, which Winton opened in his inconspicuous home in Hampstead Heath after his return from Prague in 1939.

Winton's mother also helped with her son's project. Although there were only three workers, they created the impression that theirs was a very reliable and legitimate institution.

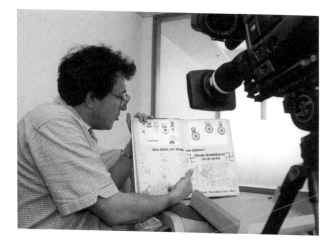

I had a precious book in front of me. To me, it could not have been more valuable if it had been made of gold. The rescue mission came to life before my eyes as if I were seeing it in a movie. I read with suspense how Winton tried to find other countries

Winton's London office, 1939

Winton's mother in the office, 1939

that might accept the endangered children. He wrote urgent letters to the leaders of many countries, saying, "Please help rescue the children of these unfortunate people!"

He even wrote a letter to the President of the United States, Franklin D. Roosevelt, from whom he received a very polite reply stating that current legislation would not permit the U.S. to help. Winton finally realized that no country other than Britain

THE FOREIGN SERVICE
OF THE
UNITED STATES OF AMERICA

AMERICAN EMBASSY

1 Grosvenor Square,
London, W. 1.
June 7, 1939.

Dear Sir:

I desire to acknowledge the receipt of your letter of May 16, 1939 addressed to the President of the United States on the subject of refugee children of Czechoslovakia.

would be willing to accept any of the children. He had to be satisfied with what was available to him.

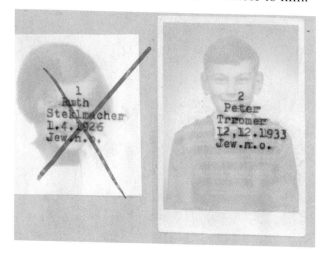

What caught my eye in the scrapbook were hundreds of cards, each bearing the photographs of eight children. The cards were covered with a transparent paper, on which Winton had written the names of the children. Some of the names were crossed out. "What did that mean?" I asked myself.

London
Winton's office
February 1939

When Winton returned to London in 1939, he brought with him a list of children who he believed were most at risk. The list contained 1,000 names. He asked the parents of these thousand children to send him their best photographs, which he then pasted onto small cards, eight photographs per card. Some parents also sent their children's drawings,

Children's drawings often helped convince families to take them in.

or wrote about their children's skills and talents, including their musical abilities or mathematics and language skills.

Winton sent these cards all over Britain, turning to refugee organizations, as well as to the publishers of pictorial magazines. In short, he sent the information

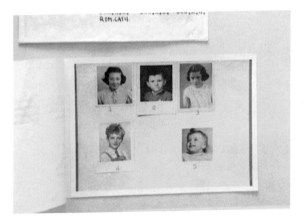

to anyone who could be of help or might be interested.

For instance, when a family from Edinburgh expressed an interest in adopting a ten-year-old girl, Winton would send them a dozen cards with photographs of ten-year-old girls.

He did not even hesitate to go door-to-door with his photographs. He found homes for many children this way. "Make your selection!" he would suggest. His system may seem rather insensitive, but it was quick, and, most importantly, it worked.

For the people of Britain, however, the decision to adopt a child was not an easy one to make. The country was in a crisis of great economic uncertainty, and the British people sensed that they were heading into war. Taking in a child was, monetarily, a significant burden. Moreover, the British Home Office required a guarantee of 50 British Pounds for each child, which at the time was a considerable amount of money. Winton himself had to pay for and organize the children's transportation. While in

Britain, he asked for assistance from noble-minded and generous people, charitable organizations, and individual sponsors.

His work was very trying. "The parents cried when they were told that their child had not been selected, but they also cried when they were told that their child had been selected!" Winton explained. "Mothers did not want to part with their young children, and the children were reluctant to leave the arms of their parents."

Often, quite unexpected situations occurred. For instance, a family would select a child for foster-care, but would not select his or her sibling, simply because the sibling seemed to be too old or did not have hair as pretty as the chosen child. In this way, good-byes at the train station in Prague were often more difficult and moving when the children had to leave their brothers and sisters behind. Having a sibling for a travel partner would have eased the pain of departure, but the decision to adopt a child was entirely voluntary, and families were not required to take both siblings.

Indeed, people are only human. Some families chose to take in a child because they needed help around the house; others had no idea how to understand and deal with children. Fortunately, these were exceptional cases, as most foster parents were good and decent people who knew how to care properly for children.

Israel
Yad Vashem Memorial
May 1998

Not until I reviewed the documents in Israel did I realize the importance of Winton's business savvy. At the time, it was not enough to be good-hearted and mean well; one had to be able to organize and implement a plan. Winton had worked at the London Stock Exchange. He was a businessman, heart and soul. He knew that one must adopt a businesslike attitude, even in charitable work.

The fundamental rule of business is that if you want to sell something, you must make it attractive through advertising. So, Winton decided to "advertise" the children for whom he wanted to find foster homes. He decided to have cards printed with the children's pictures, which turned out to be a stroke of genius. If

someone simply asks people if they are interested in adopting a Czech child, it is easy for them to say "no." On the other hand, if someone were to ask you the same question and offer to show you photographs of the children, you probably would look out of sheer curiosity. Perhaps, then, a picture of a girl or boy would catch your eye and tug at your heart.

When the foster parents selected a child, Winton marked their photograph with a large "X" or the word "Placed," meaning that the particular child had been placed in foster care. The photo cards were, of course, reusable and were circulated from one prospective family to another. It was an ingenious plan at a time when neither fax machines nor photocopiers existed.

When I held these photo cards in my hands, chills ran down my spine. On some cards, two photographs were crossed out, on others three, on another only one, and there were many on which none of the photographs were crossed out. I knew very well that those children whose photographs were not crossed

POST OFFICE TELEGRAM

Prefix. Time Handed in. Office of origin and service instructions. Words.

RECEIVED		No: 12 MRH 39 N.W.8
	90 1850 12 PRAHA URGENT	
	= URGENT=WINTON 20 WILLOW RD HAMPSTEAD LONDON=	
	=TRANSPORT POSTPONED PROBABLY TUESDDAY=	
/:	=CHADWICK=	
Telegrams for all countries in the world and radio		

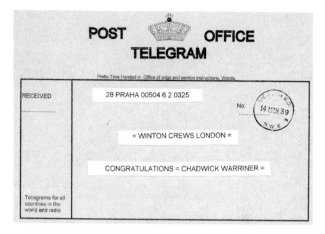

POST ☂ OFFICE
TELEGRAM

Prefix. Time Handed in. Office of origin and service Instructions. Words.

RECEIVED	28 PRAHA 00504 6 2 0325	No:	14 MCH 39 N.W. 6

= WINTON CREWS LONDON =

CONGRATULATIONS = CHADWICK WARRINER =

Telegrams for all
countries in the
world and radio

out had simply had bad luck. In this lottery of life, they had not been selected, and so they perished.

"Why was this child chosen and not that one?" I asked myself. I thought about how unjust life was and how senselessly cruel it can be. When I later spoke to Nicholas Winton about my thoughts, he told me that he had had no time to contemplate life just then. He knew that he was fighting against time, that every day counted, and that he could not afford to be emotionally engaged. Unlike everyone else, he was keenly aware that war was imminent.

Among the clippings in the book were also telegrams. They testify to how difficult it was to organize a train from Prague's main train station. Always at the last moment, something was lacking (documents, for instance, or more money), and the train was unable to leave. In a telegram sent on March 12, 1939, Chadwick, who worked for Winton at the Prague end, informed him, "Transport postponed. Probably Tuesday."

Two days later, on March 14, Winton's office in London received a telegram confirming his success: "Congratulations! Chadwick Warriner." This short message is of huge historic significance, as March 14 was the date of the first children's transport from Prague to England. The train had left only a few hours before the Germans succeeded in occupying the remainder of the Czech territories. After the success in Sweden, this was another major triumph

for Winton. He had proven that a strong will and a fierce conviction can do the impossible.

It is difficult today to imagine how painful it was for parents to part with their children at the Wilson station in Prague. There were a lot of fears and tears among the children, but also a sense of innocent, childish pleasure that they were embarking on a great adventure.

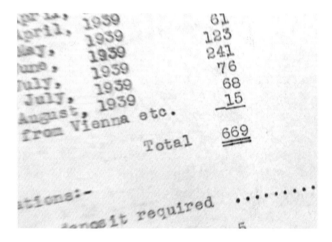

Children with numbered tags hanging around their necks boarded the train. Some couldn't turn away from their loved ones and tearfully asked, "Why are you sending me away? Don't you love me anymore?"

One mother couldn't make up her mind whether to let her little daughter go. Three times she pulled her through the window and off the train, and three times she put her daughter back on the train. Finally, the train left with the little girl on board, and she was saved.

After the first train left in March 1939, seven more trains departed, the last leaving on August 2, 1939. In total, 669 children escaped from Nazi-occupied Bohemia, Moravia, and the Slovak State!

Washington
National Archives
November 1998

I was constantly wondering what heartbreaking scenes there must have been at Prague's Wilson station on the days the children left for England. How would I represent this in my film? I called Winton at his home in England and asked if he had any photographs from that period. "We did not have time to think about photographs," he replied. "You must remember that all our activities were quickly and secretly taking place behind the backs of the German Gestapo." As if I had jogged his memory, however, Winton suddenly recalled that one of the departures was filmed by a newsreel crew. Their material might be suitable for my film, but he had never seen it. It piqued my interest.

"Was it a Czech crew?" I asked

"No, no," he returned, "They spoke English. They may have been from the United States."

"Where in the States? After all, America is a huge country!" I pressed him for the details.

"I have no idea," he replied.

"Well then," I asked dejectedly, "How am I supposed to find the newsreel? It would be like looking for a needle in a haystack!"

Winton, in his usual way, shrugged it off. "If you think that it is important, why don't you at least try to find it?" Again, I realized that, for Nicholas Winton, no hurdle was insurmountable. If it had not been for his challenge, however, I would have given up my search at once. I had little hope of finding a tiny piece of evidence in the entire United States. Nonetheless, I had been infected by Winton's eternal optimism, and decided to start making plans to cross the ocean.

I made a reservation at the National Archives in Washington, DC, the largest library in the United States of America. I requested to see all items related to Czechoslovakia and World War II.

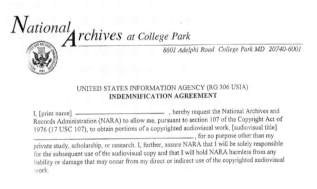

National Archives at College Park

8601 Adelphi Road College Park MD 20740-6001

UNITED STATES INFORMATION AGENCY (RG 306 USIA)
INDEMNIFICATION AGREEMENT

I, [print name] —————————————— , hereby request the National Archives and Records Administration (NARA) to allow me, pursuant to section 107 of the Copyright Act of 1976 (17 USC 107), to obtain portions of a copyrighted audiovisual work, [audiovisual title] ——————————————————————— , for no purpose other than my private study, scholarship, or research. I, further, assure NARA that I will be solely responsible for the subsequent use of the audiovisual copy and that I will hold NARA harmless from any liability or damage that may occur from my direct or indirect use of the copyrighted audiovisual work.

I was astonished by the huge quantity and variety of material that they had about my country from the 1930s and 1940s. I was given photographs, newspapers, and periodicals from the World War II period to review. For an entire week, day after day, I read everything I could get my hands on. I unpacked endless boxes of films and settled in to watch them all. Although I had intended to see the sights and reserved a room in a hotel right across the street from the White House, I never found the time to visit it. The only "sights" I saw were the interiors of subways and buses, and, of course, my piles and piles of archived documents.

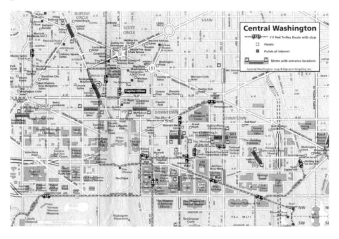

By the seventh and last day of my visit, I had lost all hope of finding the material for my film. There were so many boxes left to look through, and I didn't have enough money to stay another week. In despair I thought, "Why did I travel so far in hope of a miracle? I knew from the start that it would be nearly impossible to find that newsreel. Winton may have been right when he said, 'When there's a will, there's a way,' but that doesn't apply to me!" Nevertheless, I popped in the very last film I had time for.

"I must be seeing things," I said to myself, because it seemed to me that Winton's face had just flashed upon the screen. I rubbed my eyes in disbelief and got up to get another cup of coffee.

When I returned with an extra-large cup, I saw him again! Fortunately, as the tape rewound, I found that I wasn't hallucinating. Here was the 29-year-old Winton at Prague's Wilson station in 1939—and he was surrounded by children and their parents!

The newsreel showed scenes of excited children, who never thought for a moment that they were seeing their parents for the last time. The parents were trying to hide their tears and anguish from their young ones, while assuring them that they were going on a vacation to England, and that their families would soon follow. Winton appeared in two shots. In one,

he is smiling and holding one of the children in his arms. In the other, he is having a discussion with a group of parents.

I could not believe what I was seeing—I thought it was a miracle! I had actually found the needle in

the haystack. There may be something in Nicholas Winton's theories after all!

The staff at the National Archives had no idea what a treasure they owned. To their knowledge, an American newsreel team had shot the film in Prague while documenting general goings-on in Europe.

When Germany attacked Poland, however, the crew rushed to the battlefields to cover the emerging war. The footage on Winton then became old news. It had remained untouched in the archives for sixty years, until I asked to see it.

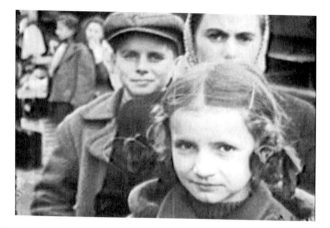

One more surprise was waiting for me in the United States—I was going to meet the renowned Czech film director Jiří Weiss! His films included *Life at Stake; The Key Man; Romeo, Juliet and Darkness;*

My meeting with Jiří Weiss in the U.S. It was like a gift from heaven!

and *Murder Czech Style*. He left Czechoslovakia in the 1960s to live in exile in the United States. He asked me what I was working on, and I told him the story of the rescued children.

"Come visit me," he said. "I have something to show you that I think will be of interest to your project!"

At his home, Weiss screened for me a film that he had shot in Britain during World War II. It was

a documentary about the Czechoslovak school in Wales, which had been established by the Czechoslovak government-in-exile in Britain so that Czech and Slovak immigrant children would

not forget their native tongue. As such, many of the pupils happened to be Winton's "children."

As I watched the documentary, I was fascinated by how the children studied, sang, and played volleyball.

*The screening of the Winton documentary
in Los Angeles in 2002*

I said to myself, "This is a documentary director's dream come true! I could not ask for more authentic material."

When I later showed Weiss's documentary to some of the Winton "children," many of them recognized themselves. "For heaven's sake, that's me!" they'd cry. "And over there is Franta, and that is Vera!"

In 2002, Weiss attended the premiere of my documentary, *Nicholas Winton: The Power of Good*, at the Wiesenthal Center in Los Angeles.

Winton's daughter, Barbara, accepted the prestigious Wiesenthal prize, "Righteous Amongst Nations," on behalf of her father from the Mayor of Los Angeles,

James Hahn. The screening was attended by the presidents of all the leading Hollywood studios.

At the end of the screening, Jiří Weiss jokingly remarked, "Had I known my footage would become part of such an important film, I would have done a better job in filming it!"

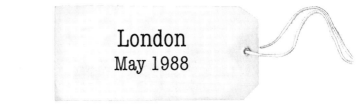

London
May 1988

Now we go to another mystery in this fascinating story. Until 1988, none of the rescued children knew who their rescuer was, a person to whom they owed their lives. This fact may sound strange, but it is true. Most of the children's parents perished during the war and never managed to tell their children how they had arrived in England. All the official documents and applications referred only to an organization called the "British Committee for Refugees from Czechoslovakia—Children's Section." This was the name Winton created for his organization, and because it was not a genuine government agency, no one else knew anything about it. For all the "children"—who were now in their seventies and eighties—knew, the organization that had helped them escape to England appeared to be similar to the Red Cross. It's possible that no one would ever have found out the real truth if Greta had not discovered the old dusty suitcase in the attic.

It was also Greta who approached Dr. Elizabeth Maxwell, the widow of media magnate Robert Maxwell, who was himself a native of Czechoslovakia. Dr. Maxwell, a leading expert on the history of the Holocaust, became extremely interested in Winton's story. Greta asked her to try to locate some of the Winton children, so that she could give them the documents that belonged to them. Dr. Maxwell recalls what happened:

Dr. Elizabeth Maxwell, 2000

"I decided to write to all the 669 addresses on Winton's list. These were the pre-war addresses of all the foster parents who had agreed to take in the children before the war began. To my great surprise, I received about 150 replies. That is how I located the first 60 Winton children. None of them had any idea about their rescuer. In fact, they told me, 'We always wanted to know who rescued us, but no one knew anything about it.'"

Dr. Maxwell then decided to contact the BBC and ask them to help her locate additional "children." Esther Rantzen, the host of the program, *That's Life,* had the brilliant idea to invite Winton and some of the rescued children to the BBC studios. No one was

The famous "Winton list" compiled in 1939

told what the program was exactly about and who was going to participate in the show. Only during the program did it gradually become obvious that the studio audience consisted of many Winton children. Just imagine, Winton, unexpectedly, and for the first time since the war, met some of the children whom he had helped to rescue. The great wave of emotion that followed was overwhelming. Winton burst into tears, as did all those around him. The viewers in their homes were also deeply affected.

The first person to be introduced to Winton during the show was the writer Vera Gissing. For many years she had searched in vain for her rescuer. She contacted various refugee organizations and spoke

From right: Sir Nicholas Winton, Esther Rantzen,
Vera Gissing, Matej Mináč, May 2007

to many rescued children. She even wrote to the
Archbishop of Canterbury, but to no avail. And now,
suddenly, she found herself sitting next to the person
who had saved her. It was the most meaningful,
most moving moment of her life. Just at that time
her book, based on diaries she had kept through the
war, was being published, and she was able to add a
few paragraphs about her rescuer to the introduction.
The title of her book was *Pearls of Childhood,* and
you will remember that this was the book I found in
1997 in the library of Prague's Jewish Museum. It
brought me such good luck and, as in a fairytale, led
me to a pot full of gold.

Vera and I became very good friends. She tirelessly
and unselfishly helped research the story of Winton's
life and rescue mission, and she was a great help
in writing the script of the film. Without Vera, and
without her investigative efforts and her books (she
has also co-written *Nicholas Winton and the Rescued
Generation*), we probably would never have heard

Vera Gissing and Matej Mináč, 2003

of Nicholas Winton! They say that stories based on real life are the most impressive ones, and this is certainly true in my case.

Prague
September 2001

The mysteries surrounding the rescue mission were now slowly unraveling. It is quite clear that Winton loves adventure, difficult tasks, and tough obstacles. When someone needs help, Winton, unlike most people, offers to help. He follows his heart, and firmly believes in being steadfast and hard headed. All one needs is not to give up!

So, when he was in Prague in 1939, Winton was not indifferent to the harsh fate that was waiting for the

Czech and Slovak children. He did not allow himself to be discouraged by people who kept reminding him that he had neither the time, nor the financial resources to save the children. Some even told him that the Gestapo would never let him reach his noble goal. Besides, where could one find a country willing to admit all these children? Winton refused to be discouraged. He was not one to give up!

The people who tried to dissuade him did not know that he was always guided by the motto, "NEVER SAY IT CAN'T BE DONE!"

Winton was also an experienced and successful businessman, and he knew how to make the most of his skills. But he never told a soul about his rescue mission and the hundreds of lives it saved. Only this one question remained unanswered: Why? Why

didn't Winton say anything about the rescue mission to anyone, not even his own wife, for fifty years?

Until recently, I could not understand it myself. Then it dawned on me: Winton could not bear to share his story because of the last transport scheduled to leave Prague on September 1, 1939. Winton recalls:

"We arranged for a transport of 251 children to leave Prague in early September. Can you imagine the scene at the train station that morning? There, the children, their parents and friends gathered to say goodbye. In

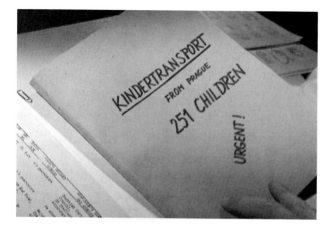

London, 250 foster parents anxiously awaited their arrival. The mothers were full of anguish, fear, and tears at the thought of sending their children into the unknown, and the children were nervous but excited to embark on such a journey. The children

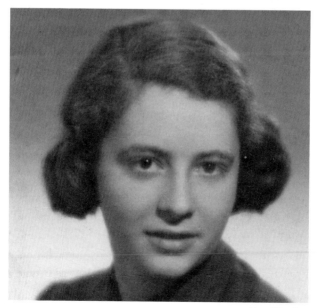

Eva Glauber

were nearly all aboard, and the train was ready to depart. But it would never leave the station. World War II had broken out, and the rescue mission jolted to a halt. None of the children on the train were ever heard from again. Their life's journey must have ended in some Nazi concentration camp…"

After many years, Winton finally admitted that he had been unwilling to speak about the rescue mission because he felt guilty that he couldn't do more for the children on the last transport. The thought that none of these children survived still haunts him today.

Věra Glauberova and her sister, Eva, were scheduled to depart on the last transport. Sixteen-year-old Eva perished in Auschwitz and her thirteen-year-old sister Věra in Riga. These photographs are all that remains.

THE LIFE OF SIR NICHOLAS WINTON

Sir Nicholas Winton was born on May 19, 1909, in West Hampstead, London. His grandparents on his father's side were German Jews who moved to the United Kingdom after their marriage in 1866, first to Manchester and later to London, where they purchased a large house. In 1907 their son, Rudolf, (Winton's father) married Barbara, who was born in Germany. She came from a highly educated family; all its members had university degrees.

Their three children—Nicholas, Robert, and Lottie— were baptized and raised in the Christian faith.

As Barbara and Rudolf were well educated, they naturally wanted their children to go to good schools.

So, they sent Nicholas and his brother Robert to Stowe, a well-known public school, to prepare them for university. Nicholas concentrated mainly on economics, but also devoted much of his time to fencing and perfected his command of the German language. Later, he became fluent in French.

Nicholas was first employed in 1928 by a commercial bank, where he was in charge of correspondence.

Nicholas Winton with his mother, Barbara, London, 1948

Later, he worked for two years in Germany, mainly for the Wassermann Commercial bank. On his return to London, he accepted a post at the Anglo-Czech bank, where he only lasted three months! He was dismissed when he complained to his supervisor that he had not been given the raise he had been promised! Nicholas gained experience at several other banks and rose to high positions, which took him all over the world.

In 1937, Winton became a member of the London Stock Exchange. That same year, he was sent on business to Johannesburg. The flight to South Africa

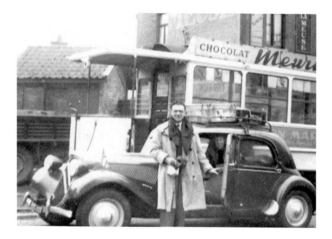

was most adventurous; it took five days, and every night was spent in a different city, such as Rome or Cairo. In those days, one could only fly in favorable weather. If the weather was bad, the passengers went sightseeing!

In 1938, Winton's last name was Wertheim. However, because they were English Christians, they didn't want to go through another war with a German

Jewish name, so they decided to change it. Nicky's friend, Stanley Murdoch, looked in a phone book for a name starting with "W," and suggested Winton. They all agreed that they liked it!

The outbreak of war in September 1939 put an end to Winton's rescue mission, which had lasted eight months. He joined the Red Cross and was sent to France.

On May 10, 1940, the German army, without warning, attacked Belgium, Luxemburg, Holland, and France. The British Red Cross, together with the British Expeditionary Force and the remnants

Winton (center) with British ambulance drivers in France, 1940

of the French Army, retreated towards the port of Dunkirk. Enemy planes constantly attacked the endless columns of vehicles, soldiers, and refugees, who were desperate to reach the sea. The road was littered with dead and injured bodies. The British High Command mobilized all seaworthy craft in

England to evacuate the troops from the French port, and they also sent all available military planes to protect those who were trying to escape the German onslaught.

Winton was one of the 224,000 British soldiers and civilians who managed to return home.

Winton (left) with his sister and brother, 1942

In 1942, Winton joined the Royal Air Force. Because of his imperfect eyesight, he was assigned, to his regret, to ground personnel. The fact that he was a fully-qualified pilot who longed to fly did not help him at all. During the war he served as a navigation officer, then in 1944 he was a navigation instructor to French pilots in La Rochelle. He reached the rank of Flight Lieutenant. Towards the end of that

Greta Gjelstrup

year he was appointed second-in-command of an RAF travelling expedition, which followed in the footsteps of the retreating German army, culminating in Prague. Incredibly, on a Czech newsreel of that

Their wedding photograph, October 1948

year, there is a shot which shows Winton introducing the latest British fighter plane!

After the end of the war, Winton joined the International Organization for Refugees and was in charge of the sale of Nazi loot found in the American occupation zone of Germany.

According to a treaty signed by five countries—Britain, France, the U.S., Czechoslovakia, and Yugoslavia—the proceeds of these sales were to be used to help the victims of the Nazis.

At the beginning of 1948, Winton joined the International Bank in Paris. There he met 29-year-old Greta Gjelstrup from Denmark, who was the secretary of the bank's director for Europe. They fell in love and, although Winton's mother objected, they married that year. The wedding took place in

October 1948, in Vejle, Denmark. They rented a flat in the Passy section of Paris and were very happy. Both of them liked to socialize, and Greta was an

excellent cook. Many friends visited them, including some famous people, such as the renowned Czech conductor Rafael Kubelík.

In 1950, the couple returned to Britain. Winton decided that he would leave the world of banking and finance. Instead, he managed an ice cream factory and later switched to the engineering industry. The Wintons purchased a house in Maidenhead, where

The Wintons with their grandchildren

Nicholas Winton with his grandchildren

their three children were born; in 1952, Nicholas; one year later, Barbara; and in 1956, Robin.

When the doctors diagnosed Robin as mentally handicapped, they recommended that he should be institutionalized. Nicholas and Greta refused to do this, because they believed that he would be better off at home – and he was. When the family reminisces about Robin, who died in 1962, they all remember him as a happy, contented child.

Nicholas built a new house for his family in which he still lives today. Thanks to Robin, he became interested in how to help mentally and physically handicapped children. He became the chairman of the local branch of MENCAP and is still a member of their National Committee. In addition, he is the president of an affiliate of Abbeyfield, an organization that builds homes for the elderly.

On one occasion, when he was 85 years old, Winton attended a festive dinner for the elderly people at one of the centers he had helped to build. He was very surprised, however, when he was mistaken for one of the residents!

Today, Winton is 98 years old. He still lives in Maidenhead near London. He gardens, cooks very well, visits the opera, plays bridge, and often travels. When asked about his interests, he says:

"I love gardening. In the past, my main physical activity was fencing. As I am too old to indulge in this sport, I use up my excess energy by growing vegetables!"

Winton is incredibly active and is nearly always in a good mood. Although his wife died eight years ago, he does not feel too lonely. He has a large family: his son Nicholas and daughter Barbara and their partners, two grandchildren, and his younger brother Robert and his wife. They all often visit him.

Nicholas Winton with the family of Tom Berman, one of the rescued children, in Israel in Kibbutz Amiad in 2004

But most importantly, Winton is so involved in his charitable activities that he could do with twice as many hours in a day! And that does not include the time he devotes to correspondence and meetings with some of the rescued children. To cope with a family of 669 members requires a lot of energy!

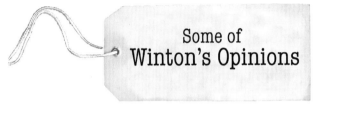

Some of
Winton's Opinions

LAUGHTER

Although on most days nothing extraordinary happens, I always try to be cheerful. Laughter is a vital part of life. I think that most people take themselves too seriously, which prevents them from acting naturally.

Nicholas Winton with Bessel Kok, a supporter of the film

NEVER GIVE UP

People so often say that something can't be done before they even try to do it, which is just an excuse to do nothing! Most things that seem impossible can actually be achieved by hard work. *I think it is the will that is often missing.*

LOVE

Ah, love! It is the one thing that is really important. It is the art of compromise, the art of co-existence; if you do not share the interests of your partner, you

The Wintons in 1998

must at least tolerate them. My wife did not mind when I left to play bridge, and I did not mind when she left to meet her girlfriends.

RELIGION

If you believe in God, then I do not understand what difference it makes if you believe as a Christian, a Jew, a Buddhist, or a Muslim. The fundamentals of all religions are basically the same: goodness, love, not to kill, and to look after your parents and those close to you. I believe people should think less about the aspects of religion that divide them and more about what these beliefs have in common, which is ethics.

ABOUT FENCING

I used to be good at fencing. Prior to the war, I represented England against Scotland. After the war, my brother Robert and I organized regional championships. We also founded the Winton Cup — an annual competition, which is now the largest fencing event in Great Britain!

Awards
given to
Sir Nicholas Winton

In October 1998, Vaclav Havel, President of the Czech Republic, presented Nicholas Winton with the Order of TGM (Tomáš Garrigue Masaryk) in recognition of his deed.

He also received the *Pride of Britain Award* for saving the 669 children.

In 1983, Queen Elizabeth II awarded Winton a MBE for his services to the community. On March 11, 2003, Winton was knighted by the Queen for his services to humanity.

It is correct to address him now as "Sir Nicholas Winton," but he is not all that interested in titles

and medals. "What can you do with them?" he asks. "Maybe you can pin them to your pajamas at night to show your wife, but otherwise they are practically good for nothing. I have never worn any of my medals."

I was surprised to learn that a minor planet, discovered in 2000 by the Czech astronomers M. Tichý and J. Tichá, was named after Winton. The Czech scientists consider Sir Nicholas Winton's deed a great example of courage and resolve.

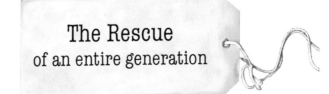

The Rescue
of an entire generation

In 1939, at the beginning of the German occupation, 118,310 Jews were living in the so-called Protectorate 140 of Bohemia and Moravia. According to the statistics, by March 15, 1945, only 3,030 of them remained, apart from the few who had not perished in Terezin or other camps.

The town of Terezin was converted during World War II into a Jewish ghetto. It became an assembly point from which most prisoners were sent further east to Auschwitz, Treblinka and other extermination camps.

More than 15,000 children went through Terezin; sadly, only about 180 of them survived.

Nicholas Winton and his team rescued 669 Czech and Slovak children and they've had children, grandchildren and even great-grandchildren! Thus he saved an entire generation. "Winton's family" now consists of more than 5,000 members.

Nicholas Winton and some of his "children" at the premiere of the feature film All My Loved Ones *in Prague, 1999*

JELINEK	Gretl.	7484	26. 3.25	Brook Lodge, Albury Heath, nr.Guildford.	Czech Section	Brit.Cttee.for Refugees from C.S.R., 5 Mecklenburg Sqr.
JELLINEK	Hans	3777	30. 5.24	near Ashford, Kent.	Agreement Czech Section	Youth Aliyah
JELINEK	Josef	3986	23.10.24	c/o Josef Jelinek, 6 Melrose Rd.S.W.18.	Miss G.C.H.Townshend, 51 Deodar Road, Putney, S.W.15.	Personal guarantee
JELLINEK	Rosa	8170	10.11.26	c/o Mr.R.A.Overton, The Green, Bilton, Rugby.	Czech Section	Czech Section
JETTER	Paul	12362	16. 9.24	Hull.	Hull Jewish Committee for Refugees, 28 Brook Street, Hull.	Personal guarantee
JOHN	Sophie	7363	15. 8.25		Dr. L. Fieldman, 10 Tollington Park, N.4.	Brit.Cttee.for Refugees from C.S.R., 5 Mecklenburgh Sqr.
JUSTITZ	Alice	5581	5. 7.23	13 Ritherdon Road, Tooting, S.W.	Woodcraft Folk,	Czech Section
KAFKA	ALICE HELENE	6171	1. 1.48			Refugee Children
KAFKA	Felix	12436	28. 6.25	Cheltenham College, evac.to Shrewsbury.	Agreement	Czech Section at Cheltenham College.
KAFKA	Georg	12435	2. 5.24	As above	Agreement	Czech Section As above
KAHN	Eva Suse	8120	27.10.23	Whittingehame Farm School.	Whittingehame Committee, 31a St.James Sqr. S.W.1.	Whittingehame Committee
KAHN	Fritz	1601	3. 7.27	Taplow School, Taplow, Bucks.	West London Synagogue, 33 Seymour Place, W.1.	Personal guarantee at Taplow School
KAHN	Gerhard	1239	29. 5.34	Carlisle	British Cttee.for Refugees from C.S.R., 5 Mecklenburgh Square,W.C.1.	Guaranteed by guarantors

Another section of the 1939 list of "Winton Children"

RECOLLECTIONS OF SOME OF THE RESCUED CHILDREN

Tom Schrecker
Publisher and Businessman
Australia

I was born in Prague on January 7, 1932. Until the time when Hitler came to power, we had no awareness of being Jewish. My father was a Czech patriot, and we were not religious. My early childhood was sadly disrupted by my parents' divorce when I was three years old.

My mother Markéta in Prague in 1935

My mother, Markéta, was a figure skater and an excellent pianist, but she had little in common with my businessman father. After their divorce, I lived for a while with my maternal grandmother in Austria, but when I was five years old, my mother placed me in a school in Merano, in northern Italy. At the time, she was living with one of the conductors of the La Scala opera in Milan. Somewhere I still have one of his conductor's batons and this, together with two photographs of my mother, are the only material objects I have left from her.

When my grandmother fell ill in Prague, we returned to Czechoslovakia. My mother looked after my grandmother, and this cost her her life. After the German occupation, she was unable to leave the country.

147

After the war, I learned through the records at the Prague Jewish museum that my mother was sent on a transport from Prague to the concentration camp of Terezin in September 1942, and from there on to an "unknown destination." This notation usually meant the concentration camp of Auschwitz, where we assume she was killed. She was 37 years old.

My father, Robert Schrecker, studied in Plzeň, worked in a bank, and became a chartered accountant. In 1929, he started his own textile wholesale business in Prague called "TEX." His offices were first in the Old Town Square, and then at 5 Pařížská Street. He was an outstanding businessman and developed a national distribution network for his fabrics based on traveling salesmen and mail order catalogues, selling cloth to tailors and directly to the public. He had a list of over 50,000 customers to whom he wrote frequently to offer new items, but also to send well wishes and birthday congratulations.

My uncle, Frank, worked for my father. This is his calling card. Later, he played a vital part in getting me to England

My father was also a keen sportsman and played soccer for the Czechoslovak national youth (under 21) team. Unfortunately, a serious elbow injury cut short his playing career, but he became a director of a leading Prague soccer club.

In 1938, at the age of six, I started elementary school in Prague. I lived with my father in an attractive apartment on Pařížská Street, near the current site of the Intercontinental Hotel. I saw little of my father, because he worked very hard in his business. Our warm-hearted cook, Katy, looked after me. I was very fond of her and met her again in 1972 during my only visit to Communist Czechoslovakia.

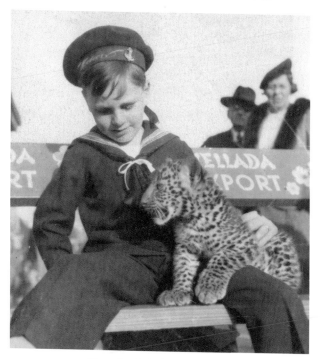

Tom, shortly before leaving Prague for England in 1939 The hand holding the cub is Katy's!

As a child, I skied in Špindlerův Mlýn in the Krkonoše Mountains north of Prague and skated on the frozen Vltava River in Prague. I loved the pastry shop near our house with its wonderful cakes and other sweets. One of my few unpleasant childhood memories is of the film *Snow White and the Seven Dwarfs*. The wicked queen gave me nightmares for quite some time!

I remember the day when the invading German army marched through Prague. It was March 15, 1939, and it was cold and snowing. People said that even the heavens were angry that such a thing could happen.

I was very attached to my father's younger brother, Frank, who played a key role in my escape. He worked for my father as a traveling salesman, but left for London after the Munich Agreement was signed in September 1938. He spoke very little English and had hardly any money. My father asked him to try to get me to England, as well.

His efforts are a good example of how important chance can be in our lives. My uncle tried several times to enter the refugee centre in London, but there were always long lines of people waiting. He had joined them for many hours without success. Finally, he decided to walk in with a briefcase as if he were working there. He looked for a foreign name on the doors in hopes of finding someone who spoke German, because his English was rudimentary, and it was unlikely that he would find a Czech-speaker. He knocked on one such door and entered to face two rather startled ladies who wanted to send him away. However, he pulled out my photograph and pleaded for their help. One of the ladies, who turned out to be the head of the center and was just briefly visiting a colleague, took pity on him. She said that she had a friend who had already adopted two boys but had expressed an interest in taking in a refugee child.

This noble lady was named Jean Barbour, and she became my guardian. She paid the required guarantee of £50 — quite a lot of money at that time — and waited for me at London's Liverpool Street Station with my uncle. I arrived on the fifth Winton train on June 3, 1939. My father had arranged for my baptism as a Roman Catholic in Prague as an extra precaution, and also possibly at Miss Barbour's request.

The journey did not cause me any trauma. I thought

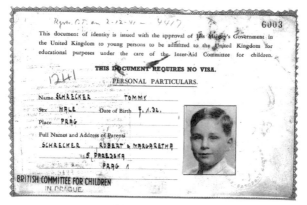

My travel permit to enter Great Britain

I was going on vacation and was looking forward to it. Moreover, I was very independent for a seven-year-old boy. I remember that when we boarded the ship for England at the Hook of Holland, I asked when it was due to leave and went ashore to buy some chocolates. When I returned in good time, I could not understand why everyone was so upset. They thought that I'd gotten lost!

After my arrival in London, our first stop was at the zoo, because I loved animals, and then we drove to Oxford where my guardian lived. Her two adopted boys were waiting for us – one was two years younger than I, and the other ten years older. Like them, I immediately began to call Miss Barbour (she never married) "Marnie." Later she adopted yet another

Jean Nelson Babour — "Marnie"

orphan, a three-year-old boy whose father was a Polish fighter pilot killed in the Battle of Britain.

From the beginning, Marnie knew how to deal wih me. At the first meal, I refused to eat. I had been spoiled and was accustomed to being persuaded. Marnie simply removed my plate and told me that the next meal would be in the evening. Naturally, I ate everything at the evening meal and since then no one has ever had a problem getting me to eat!

A bit later, as an eight-year-old, I surprised her with my budding business spirit. Once when Marnie was away, I tore up all the lead lines that were used to mark the tennis court. With a small forge I made toy soldiers, painted them, and sold them to an Oxford shop. With the money, I bought a large supply of comics. Sadly, Marnie threw out all my comics before I had the time to read most of them. As punishment, I had to paint the tennis court lines (in place of the lead ones) every time anyone wanted to play!

Marnie always encouraged us to read good books, but she never considered comics to be "good reading." We were frequently in contact with interesting people. One of her friends who lived nearby was Professor J. R. R. Tolkien, author of *Lord of the Rings*. We met him quite often and Marnie was pleased that I enjoyed his books.

Whenever any of us caught one of the then prevalent children's diseases (such as mumps or measles), Marnie put us all into same room so that we would, if possible, all catch the illness at the same time! That was not so bad, but worse was that we always had to go to bed at 6:30 in the evening. This meant that, when we went to the cinema (there was no TV in those days), we sometimes couldn't stay until the end of the film. It was only much later that I went to some of those films to see how they ended.

I was very lucky that I had my uncle in England, and he visited me quite often. When I later began to study at boarding schools, he sent me care packages. We had enough food at those schools, but there was not much variety, and British boarding schools, especially during the war years, were not famous for their good cooking. My uncle Frank later opened an old master paintings gallery in the fashionable center of London, and it is thanks to him that I became an avid collector of art. Later in the war he married and had a daughter. I'm in touch with her daughter, who lives in New York and is, as far as I know, my only living blood relative. Unfortunately, as neither she nor I have any children, we are both likely to end our family lines.

My wartime guardian, Marnie, was born in Edinburgh to a very distinguished Scottish family. Amongst her ancestors were Robert the Bruce and the Royal Stuarts. Her father was president of the Royal College of Physicians and co-author of the famous *Manual of Gynaecology,* which was the first scientific, modern textbook on women's medicine. Her grandmother, a member of the Nelson publishing family, was married to George Brown, who is known as "the father" of the Canadian Parliament. Her cousins' estate near Pitlochry includes a waterfall that Queen Victoria liked to visit. In short, a remarkable family!

Marnie studied at Oxford University and later

became active in many social causes. She also converted to Roman Catholicism, and was one of the few people I have known who really lived by their religious faith. When we went to Italy soon after the war, we were at Naples railway station when we discovered that we had lost all our passports, tickets, and money. Marnie suggested that we kneel down and pray. Almost immediately, a man approached us and asked us whether we needed help. It turned

Tom with Uncle Frank, Marnie, and his beloved dog, in Oxford in 1940. (In the background is John, Marnie's adopted son who is two years younger than Tom)

out that he worked at the British Embassy in Rome, and he arranged everything for us. Marnie was convinced that our prayers saved us. In spite of her wonderful example, I have never been religious, though I recognize that religious faith can bring much consolation to people.

I also experienced the war more directly. At Easter 1941, we were staying at a seaside resort in the south of England. One night, there was a German air attack. The bombs may have been dropped by mistake, but after the raid, few of the houses on our street remained standing. Fortunately, ours was one of them!

Late in 1942, we moved to a farm in the north of Scotland, near Elgin, because Marnie felt it would be healthier for us children. It certainly was not a luxury farm, and we had to help with all the chores. However, I have wonderful memories of that time. We sold our milk and other produce. I had a dog, a Great Dane that I loved very much. We had brought him from Oxford and, because I was still quite small, I could ride on his back. He was my constant companion. Unfortunately, while I was away at boarding school, he ate some chicken bones that splintered in his stomach and died. I was heartbroken! However, most children are resilient and, after Marnie gave me a Shetland pony, I eventually got over it.

There were many enjoyable things to do. We played golf and tennis. With one of my "stepbrothers," I once sailed as far as Ireland in an Aberdeen fishing trawler. After we finished our morning chores on the farm, we were free to roam the surrounding moors. Occasionally, I followed the local hunt on my pony. We had the entire top floor of a barn as our "kingdom." We entered by a rope ladder through a trapdoor and required a secret password. In short, it was an idyllic time for us children, although the world was in the midst of a terrible war.

Sadly, Marnie died quite young from cancer in early 1951. Almost to the end, she never let us know how seriously ill she really was. It was typical of her selfless nature that she did not want to cloud our happy childhood. She lived by her Christian ideals and was the most wonderful example and inspiration for all the children she adopted and looked after.

Unlike the majority of the other Winton children, I had the enormous good fortune that at least one of my parents survived the war. My father managed to get to England in 1942, but only after very dangerous events. Late in 1939, one of his employees, who wanted to take over my father's business, falsely reported to the Nazi authorities that he had made derogatory remarks about Hitler. My father was imprisoned in the Pankrác jail in Prague, and it seemed that his fate was hopeless. However, his courageous secretary, Marie Krejčová, did something that in the context of the time was quite incredible.

Tom with his father in 1939 and in 1943

She went to the Gestapo headquarters and told them that it was a false accusation. Amazingly, after two months my father was released. He had to turn over his business to a Nazi appointee and pay a large fine, but he escaped with his life. Two photographs indicate the effect of his imprisonment. When he went to jail, he had brown hair. When he came out, his hair was white.

My father now desperately tried to get out of German-occupied Bohemia and Moravia. One of the last places still willing to accept refugees was Shanghai in China. The route via Italy was still open and my father embarked at Genoa on the ship S.S. Conte Verdi. They were in the Suez Canal on June 10, 1940, when Italy joined the war on the side of Germany. The ship's captain was ordered to return

Robert and Trude Schrecker's wedding in London in 1946

to Italy, which would have been a catastrophe for the refugees on board. They threatened mutiny and, fortunately, the captain agreed to proceed to Shanghai!

On the journey, my father met his future wife, Trude Engel, who was very beautiful and accomplished. Her story is another example of the important part that luck and chance can play in life. Trude, with her parents and elder brother, left their home in Bratislava for Prague to pick up their exit papers. There, her father became ill and the family did not want to leave him. It sounds awful to say so but mercifully, after some months, he. died, and this saved the lives of the rest of the family. Even if he had just lived one extra week, they would have been unable to get out through Italy and would probably have ended up in concentration camps two years later.

In Shanghai, Trude and her family survived by making artificial flowers. Meanwhile, my father, who was a mathematical genius, made his living by developing a probability system for betting on the game of Jai-Alai (like the Spanish Pelota). He did very well, because the Chinese are great gamblers.

In 1942, my father managed to get to England. Because he was on his own and starting a business from scratch, I continued to spend my holidays with Marnie. However, I saw my father regularly. He worked incredibly hard, so he often left me in a cinema. I almost remember some of the films by heart, because I saw them three times on the same day! Once again, he showed that he was an outstanding businessman. He cornered the field in plastic (PVC) sheeting remainders—buying all the leftovers from the large manufacturers and selling them cheaply to many (mainly refugee) small businesses. Thus, he again became wealthy, though he started in

England with nothing. He also became a great fan of English soccer. He and Trude, who joined him from Shanghai in 1946, hardly missed an English international match anywhere in the world. After a while, they became great friends of the English team management, and my father was often invited to sit with the manager on the trainer's bench!

After the war, my father considered returning to Prague, but his business there was gone and he was doing very well in London by then. Moreover, he was worried by the political developments in Czechoslovakia, which led to the Communist takeover in February 1948. Although we did not return, my father remained a faithful supporter of Czechoslovak soccer and whenever the national teams came to England, he did everything possible to help them.

Tom during officer training at Eaton Hall near Chester, England, 1951

Tom as a student at Oxford in 1952

Today, I regret that I did not develop a closer relationship with my father. We loved each other and corresponded regularly, but our long separation and our different educations stood between us. He later died tragically. To this day, I am sorry that I did not ask him many questions about his life and my childhood.

I mainly went to boarding schools. Altogether, I attended eleven schools! I did my two years of

Tom with his business colleagues in New Delhi, India, 1962

national service in the British Army as an infantry officer based in Germany.

After that, I went to Oxford University, where I had won a scholarship in history at University College.

From 1955, I devoted myself fully to a business career. I started by working in London for the American publisher of Reader's Digest. I helped them set up distribution arrangements in over fifty countries. I travelled all over the world for twelve

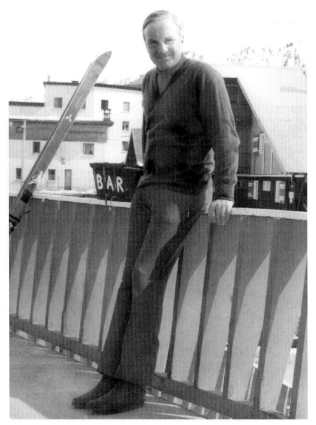

Tom in Val d'Isère, 1972

years and met many interesting people. Then I moved to Australia, where I founded a direct marketing publishing company in partnership with a major U.K. publisher. After I sold this business, I returned for a while to Reader's Digest in New York and Hong Kong. Later I helped to start the Harlequin romantic novel publishing company in France. After that, I founded a cosmetics company in Australia with British partners. I sold this company in 1990 and retired.

I have had a very eventful and interesting life, but everything has its price. My involvement with business and the enormous amount of travel did not help me to start a family, and I have remained alone.

Today I spend most of the northern winter skiing in Val d'Isère, France, and helicopter skiing in western Canada.

Trude Schrecker, my stepmother, with Nicholas Winton at the London premiere of the film All My Loved Ones *in 2000*

For the rest of the year, I split most of my time between Australia, England, and the Czech Republic. I particularly love Třeboň in southern Bohemia. There are also some veteran tennis tournaments, music festivals, and treks all over the world. So my peripatetic fate continues! I enjoy recording these travels in scrapbooks with thousands of photographs and still collect paintings and old English silver.

As a child, I naturally spoke Czech as well as German and some Italian. I forgot all these languages after I arrived in England. Later, my father helped me learn French in France and German in Austria. Now I am studying Czech, so it is something of a paradox that I am learning my mother tongue at an advanced age!

Like the majority of those who were saved by Sir Nicholas Winton, I also try to help other people. I consider my survival as a debt I must repay to the world. So, I support a number of charitable

L to R – Above: Tom, Vera Gissing, Barbara Winton, Nicholas Winton, translator Doris Kožíšková. Below: Matej Mináč with his wife, Karin, and Martina Štolbová in Prague, 2002

organizations. I believe that the greatest problems in the world today are the population explosion in many countries and the lack of tolerance in many societies. Our future depends on finding answers to these questions.

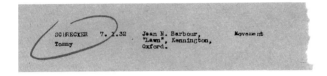

SCHRECKER   7. I.32   Jean N. Barbour,   Movement
Tommy   "Lawn", Kennington,
                          Oxford.

Vera Gissing
(Diamantová)
Author, Great Britain

As a young child I lived in Čelákovice, a little town not far from Prague, and I had a very happy life. My sister Eva was elegant and very clever, in short everything I was not. But I had wonderful parents and I loved them dearly. There was not a cloud in my sky.

Everything changed after September 1938, when Germany seized the Czechoslovak border region. I will never forget a little refugee girl from the Sudetenland who joined our class. Her family had to flee in such a hurry that she brought hardly any clothes with her. Her father pulled her out of bed in her pajamas in the middle of the night and wrapped her in a blanket. When she came to school, she didn't even have shoes on, and that really shocked me. I remember that during recess I ran home and brought her a pair of my shoes. I was worried that my mother might be angry, but when I confessed what I had done, she hugged me and said, with tears in her eyes, "Bring Anna home with you when school is over and let us see what other clothes we can find for her."

But soon dark clouds also began to gather above us, too. I will never forget March 15, 1939, the

Vera with her father and older sister

day German troops occupied what remained of our country. I woke up to the sound of German soldiers marching into our square. I was more excited than afraid, until their commandant decided to occupy the best room in our house. When he ordered my father that we must speak only German from then on, father turned to him and said, "No, we shall speak Czech, and German only in your presence."

Irma and Karel Diamant, 1939

167

The commandant then stood up and spat in father's face. I will never forget the saliva running down his cheek.

One evening during supper, mother said quietly that Eva and I would be going to England at the end of June. Father's face suddenly looked shocked and old. He did not speak, but buried his face in his hands; when he looked up, there were tears in his eyes. He sighed and whispered, "All right, let them go."

Before our departure, my parents gave me two wonderful gifts. The first was a beautiful, leather-bound book full of blank pages. "Use it as your diary," my father told me. "I want you to write in it what you are doing, what you're thinking, if you're homesick or happy, so that when you come back to us, we can sit around the table and read the diary together."

On my last night at home, my mother took me to an open window. The sky was full of stars. She said, "There will be times when you'll feel lonely and homesick. Let the stars of the night and the sun of the day be the messengers of our thoughts and love. Then we will always be close."

Soon we were standing on the station platform. The last embrace, the last words of love and hope. I still remember the pain on my parents' faces as the train began to move. Until that moment they had managed to conceal their anguish.

Steam covered everything. It looked like the morning mist, and I could not take in what was happening around me. All I saw were the faces of my beloved mother and father as the train took us farther and farther away. How thankful I was to have Eva at my side!

After a two-day journey, we arrived at London's Liverpool Street Station. We were a large group, several hundred children in all!

We were taken into a big hall where we sat on chairs arranged in long rows. Name after name was called and child after child got up and left with the person

Vera's foster-family chose her after seeing this photograph

who came to collect them. Then Eva's turn came, too, and I was left sitting there all alone with my backpack. I felt so lost and so afraid! Suddenly a little lady, not much taller than I, came into the hall. She ran toward me with tears and laughter and gave me a big hug. She said some words I did not understand at the time, but they were "YOU SHALL BE LOVED!" And loved I was.

When I arrived, my foster-mother was 30 years old, but already then she had a weak heart and had to rest a lot. I found it hard to keep quiet, as I was by nature somewhat noisy and rather wild, and so I often had to be reprimanded. But I am happy to say, that all that resting stood Mummy Rainford (as I was asked to call her), in good stead, because even with her weak heart she lived to be 103!

Years later, when I asked my foster-father why they chose me, he said, "I knew I could not save the world; I knew I could not stop the war coming; but

The Rainfords—Vera's foster-parents

Vera Gissing with her rescuer

I knew I could save one human life. As the British Prime Minister Chamberlain broke his promise to Czechoslovakia, and as Jews were most in danger, I decided I had to help a Czech Jewish child."

Until 1988, I had no idea to whom my sister and I owed our lives. Then unexpectedly, I was invited to participate in a BBC television program, *That's Life,* where, to my immense joy, I came face to face with the man who had saved us.

Even today, many years later, I cannot find words to describe how I felt. And imagine my surprise when I discovered that Nicholas Winton, my savior, lives just a few miles from me!

We quickly became good friends. Nicky often comes for lunch and many times we are joined by other Winton children who want to meet him. I have become his spokeswoman, secretary and the buffer between him and the media. I have researched the story of his rescue mission extensively and am now

171

*"Christening" the Slovak edition of Pearls of Childhood
in Bratislava, 2002*

the person to whom the people who are looking
for information about Nicky can turn to. During
my career as a writer I have translated, edited, and
rewritten about 40 books. I'm the author of several
books for children. My autobiography, *Pearls of
Childhood*, has been published many times in Britain,
and also in the U.S., Germany, Slovakia, the Czech
Republic and Japan.

Matej Mináč has written in this book that *Pearls
of Childhood* was "the treasure" on which all his
films about Winton are based. He was also pleased
to have my latest book, *Nicholas Winton and the
Rescued Generation,* co-written with my friend, the
late Muriel Emanuel.

I often think of the kindness, generosity, and
compassion the Rainfords displayed when they
made me part of their family. Together with
Nicholas Winton, they saved not only my life but
also the lives of my children, grandchildren, and all
the generations to come.

I also want to contribute something to the world, and so I often give talks in British schools and universities and share with them the experiences described in my books. But most importantly, I highlight the deed of Nicholas Winton.

Once when I was talking to a young group of children, I wanted to stress the importance of being loved. "Be happy that you have parents who love you.

Vera's foster-mother, Mrs. Rainford, 2002

"You don't realize how much that means. Even if you have just one parent, the important thing is that you are loved." Then I told them how I lost my family.

"But my parents are with me to this day, for no one can take away my memories of the ten happy years I spent with them. We must learn to count our blessings no matter how thin they are, instead of complaining about what is missing in our lives."

As soon as I finished, a seven-year-old girl from India approached me. "Please, can I hug you?" she

173

asked. "You see, my parents are getting divorced. I thought they didn't love me any more because now I have to live at this boarding school and I really felt rejected." Then she smiled and added, "After your talk I am sure that mum and dad do love me, though we don't live together anymore. And I will learn to count my blessings."

I thought then how fortunate I was to have kept my diaries and my parents' letters, and in doing so was able to publish my story – an authentic testimony not only of what was evil, but of the goodness of Man and the strength of the human spirit. From the hundreds of letters I have received from adults, teachers, and children of all ages, I realize I am keeping the memory of my parents alive, perhaps forever. How proud they would have been that the story is helping to educate the young people of today, as well as the adults! It proves that good can come out of evil and that all of us, young or old, can do our best to make our world a better place.

I would like to tell you one more story from my youth. When I was sixteen and at the Czech school in Wales, I fell in love for the first time with a handsome boy named Walter. We were both young and so innocent! We went for walks and held hands. When he first kissed me, I was in seventh heaven. I really loved him. However, he spoke Czech badly and was not one of our headmaster's favorites, as he resented Walter for being partly German and for going out with such a pure Czech girl! Finally, he made Walter leave the school. However, we wrote to each other frequently. Soon after the war ended,

I returned to Prague, although I knew my parents had perished. I thought Walter would contact me, but the years went by and I did not hear from him. I discovered what had happened only a few years ago. Walter had learned of the fate of my parents and, in a way, he felt guilty because of his mother's German origins. He thought I would not want to know him. Then, in 1998, he happened to meet a mutual friend from our wartime school, who gave Walter my address. He was afraid to call me at first, but in the end he did and so, after so many years, our friendship was renewed.

Vera Gissing with Walter after nearly 60 years

Walter and his wife, Anita, have visited me several times now, and we have been the best of friends ever since. Walter told me that when he asked Anita to marry him, he said, " I have loved only two women in my life, you and a girl named Vera Diamant. I will never stop loving Vera, but I promise I will always love you more." Then he showed her my photograph, which was still in his wallet, and told her the full story. Anita was so moved that when their daughter was born, she insisted on naming her Vera after me.

The story of Nicholas Winton gives hope to our turbulent world in which terrorism, mass killings, and the suffering of innocent refugees are daily events. Nicky showed us what a single "ordinary" person can achieve if he really wants to help.

It is a challenge to all of us.

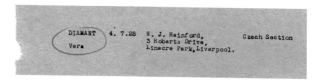

DIAMANT   4. 7.28   R. J. Rainford,   Czech Section
Vera   3 Roberts Drive,
                      Linacre Park,Liverpool.

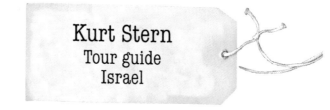

Kurt Stern
Tour guide
Israel

When I was a child, my entire family often used to visit the town of Karlovy Vary (Carlsbad). I remember it better than my native town of Chodov. Every Sunday afternoon we would go for tea and dancing at the Grand Hotel Pupp, a landmark hotel right on the spa promenade in Karlovy Vary. There we experienced the remnants of the good life of Central Europe of the thirties, before the birth and spread of Nazism.

Apart from memories, I don't have much from my childhood—a few photographs taken before my departure for England, where I was adopted by the Nunn family, and my mother's toiletries case. It has

Kurt Stern's young family

177

accompanied me everywhere I've gone during the last 60 years. There is a small piece of soap in it that still has a slight smell to it.

I preciously guard my father's gold watch, which will one day belong to my son. I am very grateful to my mother for finding the courage to send me into the unknown. All the rest of my family who stayed in the Czech lands perished.

Kurt Stern's large family got together during the filming of the documentary in 2000

Years later, I went to Israel to fight in the War for Independence. There, I met my wife and settled down. For many years I worked in hotels as a pastry chef, but for the last 24 years, I have worked as a tour guide. I have a son and a daughter, a son-in-law, a daughter-in- law, and four grandchildren.

STERN   12. 4.29   W. R. Nunn,   Movement
Kurt   Street Farm, Redg
                      Diss, Norfolk.

Hugo Marom
Airport Builder
Israel

I remember a day when the Germans occupied the country in March 1939 that the schools in Brno ordered their pupils to go outside and line the sidewalks. Suddenly students from the German school came out in their leather short pants and white socks and cheered for the German occupiers. I remember seeing Hitler in an open car. He was standing straight and looked ahead—neither to the right nor to the left. Already then, although still a child, I felt very anxious and afraid.

When my family began planning for the imminent danger, I was ten years old and my name still was Hugo Meisel. Both my parents had read Hitler's book *Mein Kampf,* and they argued about whether it

Hugo Marom with his mother and younger brother, Rudy

was possible that Hitler would do to the Jews what he had written. My mother insisted that it was, but my father didn't believe it. The Meisel family had lived in the Czech lands for a thousand years and felt more Czech than Jewish and in fact more Czech than most Czechs!

But my mother had made up her mind. In the end, I left for England with my nine-year-old brother, Rudy, and three friends. We departed convinced that

Hugo Marom with his brother

our parents would follow us soon. Our transport of 68 children left from Prague station not realizing that it was the last group that would be able to leave the country.

The journey through Germany seemed endless. I recall the anxiety we felt when the German police boarded the train and the overwhelming relief when the Dutch police arrived. The Dutch seemed to us to be so much friendlier.

This feeling of great relief passed through the train like lightning. Everything suddenly looked brighter, and the carriage windows were opened for the first time. They served us white bread. I had never tasted bread like that—it tasted wet!

When we arrived at Liverpool Street station in London on August 2, 1939, no one was waiting for us. We sat on our suitcases on the station platform all day, from morning until evening, and had no idea what would happen to us. A cab driver noticed us and asked what was going on. I already spoke a little English, so I explained to him that a certain Mr. Rabinowitz was supposed to send someone to fetch us, but no one had come. Unfortunately, we had neither Mr. Rabinowitz's address, nor the address of the boarding house where we were to stay. We were very hungry and delighted when the cab driver drove us to a place where they sold fish and chips. It was our first hot meal since our departure from Prague. We spent the next two nights in the taxi driver's two-room apartment with his wife and their baby.

The following day, the taxi driver drove us up and down the East End of London looking for a Jewish boarding house, orphanage, or boarding school that would admit us. Finally, on the third day he found a German boarding house for refugee children in Cricklewood that was willing to accept us even though we were Czech. We spent several weeks there in a very unfriendly atmosphere. Fortunately, we were then transferred to Bedford where we were assigned to a foster family.

One day in 1940 during the Battle of Britain, I was

on a morning walk when an air raid warning sounded and I saw a German Heinkel aircraft. I was already able to identify different aircraft at that time.

The plane flew right over me, and I could see the bombs dropping with my own eyes. A few seconds later, a British Hurricane aircraft appeared behind the Heinkel and started firing. I was so impressed

Correspondence with my parents

that I wrote a letter to my parents that night, telling them I had decided to become either a pilot or an aeronautical engineer.

I still have that letter somewhere; regrettably, my parents never read it.

Ultimately, I did become a pilot. In November 1948, I was one of three pilots who flew Spitfire

Hugo Marom with his family in Tel Aviv, 2000

airplanes from Czechoslovakia to Israel. The Israeli government had bought these planes from the Czechoslovak Republic. At that time, no other country was willing to sell arms to Israel. I am proud to have been one of the founders of the Israeli Air Force.

When I finished my career as a pilot, I began designing airports. One of the airports I designed was the International Airport in Paraguay. Today, I am working on the design of an international airport located on an artificial island opposite Tel Aviv. It will be fantastic!

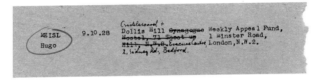

Joe Schlesinger
TV Reporter
CBC Network, Canada

I was born in 1928. We lived in the center of Bratislava, the capital of Slovakia, just below the castle that dominates the town. Bratislava was a multilingual city and all signs were in Slovak, Hungarian, and German. The town's name in Slovak was Bratislava, but also *Pozsony* in Hungarian and *Pressburg* in German.

In front of Schlesinger's store

Our parents often went to the cinema or to the theater. To this day, I have flashbacks of small details such a walk with my father to the coffee house, where I drank hot chocolate topped with lashings of whipped cream. We lived a very pleasant life.

My father owned a shop that sold cleaning products and toiletries.

Joe with his younger brother, Ernie

Then the situation in Europe began to deteriorate. Although I was still a child, I sensed that our country faced danger. We, the Jews, felt it most.

We grew up with Hitler. At first we saw him only as a distant danger and made fun of him. We imitated his Charlie Chaplin moustache and copied the strange way he combed his hair across his forehead.

We often heard Hitler screaming on the radio and watched Sudeten Germans marching and chanting: "Lieber Fuhrer, mach uns frei von der Tschechoslowakei!" (Dear Leader, liberate us from Czechoslovakia!) And this chanting was getting closer and closer to us.

I distinctly recall how one day on the way to school, I was attacked by a group of thugs from the "Hitler Jugend" (Hitler Youth). We were scared and spoke about it at length over dinner.

My parents were among those who desperately tried to get us out to safety. I recall my mother saying

Joe Schlesinger's parents

to a friend, "We are sending our boys away until the whole thing blows over." For me, traveling to England appeared to be a great adventure and we prepared well for our journey. We had English lessons from a young lady. I do not recall that we learned from her how to speak English, but to this day the song *My Bonnie lies over the Ocean* is etched in my memory. I was eleven years old and my brother Ernie was nine when, at the end of July 1939, our parents got us ready to leave for Britain. As we were coming from Slovakia, we were not

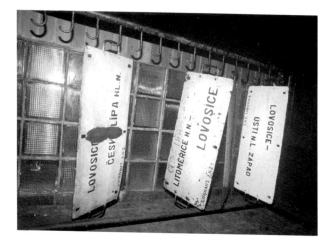

permitted to join the transport in Prague. So, we had to wait for the train from Prague in Lovosice, a border town inside the German Reich.

The train was running late and it was getting dark. The German stationmaster insisted that we had to go inside the building. In Hitler's Germany, however, Jews were not permitted in the waiting room, so he escorted us into the men's toilet.

Joe Schlesinger's father

And so I spent my final moments with my father in a smelly bathroom in the German Reich! Today, when I look at my own children, I try to imagine even a fraction of the anxiety my father must have felt at that time.

The atmosphere in the train was rather strange. Some children, including my brother, were crying, and I had to take care of my brother, because our parents had asked me to do so. For most of the others, going to England was an exciting adventure. When we left Germany and entered Holland, we received a friendly welcome. We were given hot cocoa and bread. We were used to central European rye bread, so the white bread seemed strange to us — rather like cotton wool!

When we arrived at the port of Hook of Holland, we boarded a big ship. Until then, I had only seen small steamboats in Bratislava on the river Danube. That night, as we were crossing the English Channel, the ship slowly lulled us to sleep. Suddenly, I heard

189

singing from one of the far cabins. Gradually, throughout the ship, one could hear the Czech National Anthem, *Kde domov můj, kde domov můj,* (Where is my home, where is my home). This was a question that remained unanswered for many years, and for some of us it remains unanswered to this day.

We arrived at London's Liverpool Street Station early in the morning. I don't remember the building, but I do remember something exceptional: we didn't have to go down several steps from our train to reach the station platform, because it was on the same level as our train. I was most impressed! The first night in England, my brother and I stayed in someone's home in London, but I had no idea where or whose house it was. It was not until 1990, when I held in my hands Winton's now famous scrapbook, that I noticed a letter written in familiar handwriting. It was from my mother, written in 1939 to Mrs. Winton, Nicky's mother! She wrote to thank her for taking us in that first night and said in her letter that she would never forget her kindness and generosity.

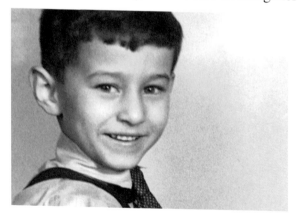

From that moment, the scrapbook, full of charts, official letters, lists of the children and columns of costs plus other documents, some even stamped by the Nazis, became precious and personal.

In 1941, I joined the Czechoslovak boarding school in Wales. My younger brother followed me later. We spent four very happy years there. Among other responsibilities at the school, it was my job to review daily news headlines. In this way, I was introduced to

journalism. One day, June 6, 1944, I was listening to the BBC. They were discussing the frequent clashes between the Allied Forces and German speedboats. That night I sat down and wrote "It appears that the Allied invasion of Europe has begun, which means that France is on her way to being liberated."

The next morning, during breakfast, my schoolmates laughed at me and said that I must have imagined it all, as no such news had been announced. However, at 9 or 10 o'clock that morning, the BBC issued a special report from the highest command of

Allied forces for Europe: *"General Eisenhower has announced that Allied forces have landed in Normandy, France."*

When war ended, I did my utmost to return to Prague as quickly as possible. I was extremely worried about the fate of my parents, so as soon as I landed, I went to a building called U Hybernů. It was a center where families that had been torn apart tried to find each other.

Joe Schlesinger after his return to Prague

Inside the building, the walls were covered with lists of names and various information. But there was not a trace of our parents. Much later, I learned that the Nazis had deported them to Poland, but to this day I don't know how they perished.

My brother and I were placed in a hostel; Ernie was subsequently transferred to an orphanage, where he was extremely unhappy. When he heard that he could emigrate to Canada, he did so immediately. A Major in the army took me in, but later it turned out that he didn't do so out of concern for me, but in order to be given a bigger flat!

After the Communist takeover in Czechoslovakia in 1948, I was in a way lost, because I had spent my childhood in England and the new regime considered this almost as a crime. Furthermore, I was working as a translator-interpreter at the Western Press Agency AP (Associated Press) and was slowly getting into journalism.

The Communists soon started arresting people from the AP's Prague office, and I realized that I must leave the country as quickly as possible. I crossed the border illegally and ended up in a refugee camp in Vienna, Austria.

In 1950, I arrived in Canada. Initially, I worked as a construction worker, a waiter, and even as a sailor. I

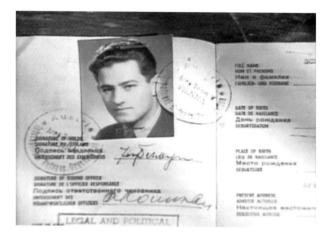

simply did whatever it took to earn a living. Later I got to the University of British Columbia. One day, by chance, I walked into the editorial offices of the university's student newspaper *Ubyssey* and was offered a job! That was the real beginning of my career as a journalist.

Since that day journalism has taken me to every corner of the world. I spent four years as a correspondent in Paris, where I met my American future wife, Mike. Both our daughters were born there. I was also a correspondent in Hong Kong, Washington and Berlin. I reported on various military conflicts

Filming the documentary about Nicholas Winton

in Indochina, Vietnam, Pakistan, Nicaragua, El Salvador, Afghanistan and Iraq.

Life has been generous to me, and I am the happiest person both in my family life and my career. I have

Joe's wife, Mike, with their daughters

195

a job that I love and I love my family. I could not wish for anything more. And I owe my happiness to Nicky Winton.

Joe Schlesinger and grandchild

Joe Schlesinger's
comments about
Sir Nicholas Winton

Winton's rescue mission is a tale of hundreds of lives. Above all, it is the story of one man, a Good Samaritan who, while on his travels, saw others in great need; his heart went out to them and he cared for them. According to the scriptures, the Good Samaritan sat a poor stranger on his horse, anointed him with oil and served him wine; he took him to an inn and looked after him.

For me and the other 668 children, the horse was the train; the oil and wine—as I recall it—were the cups of hot chocolate; the inn, where he found shelter, were the British Isles. And the Good Samaritan? A young Englishman named Nicholas Winton.

When the world around him was closing its eyes to evil, he went out of his way to do something about it. Nicky Winton is no Hector, nor some modern Achilles, he is just a decent man who was

Nicholas Winton with his granddaughter

Winton's children attending the Premiere of the documentary in Prague, 2001

not discouraged from doing the right thing by the world's indifference.

The people Nicholas Winton helped are now greyhaired grandfathers and grandmothers in their seventies, even eighties, but whatever age they are, they always will be "Nicky's children."

SCHLESINGER 14. 5.28   George Cowan,   Personal
Josef   12 Oakfield Road,
                        Gosforth, Northumbs.   guarantee

Tom Berman
World-renowned Biologist
Kibbutz Amiad, Israel

I was born in the town of Hradec Králové, but we lived in Hronov. My father was the managing director of a local textile factory, and we lived a comfortable life. I was the only child and very spoiled.

Tom with his parents

In 1939, my mother insisted on getting me out of Czechoslovakia. Indeed, she succeeded, as I was one of the 669 lucky ones who departed by train to England and thus survived.

After the war ended, I heard perhaps the only humorous story from the days of the Nazi occupation. The local photographer in Hronov had displayed a large portrait of a baby in the front window of his studio. It happened to be my portrait. The irony was

THIS DOCUMENT REQUIRES NO VISA.

PERSONAL PARTICULARS.

Name BERMANN THOMAS

Sex MALE Date of Birth 15.2.34.

Place KÖNIGGRÄTZ

Full Names and Address of Parents

BERMANN KARL & LENKA

U. NACHODA

HRONOV M/MET

COMMITTEE FOR CHILDREN IN PRAGUE.

Permit to enter Great Britain

that the caption under the portrait claimed this was the portrait of a typical Aryan child!

In Glasgow, I was taken in by a childless Jewish family, the Millers. They had originally wanted a little girl. As long as it was possible, my parents wrote to my foster parents in Glasgow. In one letter, they said, "We thank you from the bottom of our hearts for the love and care you are lavishing upon our child. We only hope that Tommy, in his child's innocence, does not take advantage of your kindness."

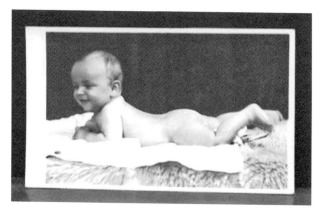

Tom's foster mother, Mrs. Miller, with Tom

At first, I was very unhappy and gave my foster family a lot of trouble. But, slowly, I adjusted. I learned English easily, and that helped me a lot. On the other hand, I just as quickly forgot my Czech. The Millers did all they could to make me feel happy and at home. They often spoke to me about my parents. So, even though I grew up away from my parents, I was raised in a loving family.

Nicholas Winton on a visit to Tom Berman
in Kibbutz Amiad in 2004

I was determined to return to my family in Czechoslovakia. However, after the war, I found out that my parents had not survived. So, I remained in Scotland, where I joined the Zionist youth movement, Habonim.

In 1952, I arrived in Israel. Since 1953, I have been a member of Kibbutz Amiad. A kibbutz is an association of people who have agreed to live in a collective settlement where they share all their belongings.

When I arrived in Israel, the Kibbutz looked quite different from the way it does now. Then, there were just a couple of barren, desolate hills. Only a person with a great imagination could have seen the way it looks today. Now it is really beautiful here. We have a prosperous community with lots of children, homes, and greenery. There are about 300 adults and 200 children. I married my wife, Debbie, and we have three daughters.

I studied microbiology for eight years in the United States and earned a doctorate. For the last thirty-five years, I have worked as a scientist on the shores of the Sea of Galilee.

I am a co-founder of a laboratory for lake research, the Kinneret Institute, which is now a world-renowned and respected research center.

Today I am retired, which leaves me time for my other passion, writing poetry. A frequent theme of my poems is my childhood, including my departure for England. This is one of my poems:

The Leather Suitcase

They don't
make suitcases
like that
any more.

Time was,
when voyage meant

train, steamship
distances unbridgeable
waiting for a thinning mail
weeks, then months
then nothing.

Time was
when this case
was made
solid, leather,
heavy stitching
with protective edges
at the corners.

Children's train,
across the Reich
stops
and starts again…

Holland
a lighted gangplank,
night ferry to grey-misted
sea-gulled Harwich
again the rails
reaching flat across
East Anglia
to London

There's the suitcase
in my bedroom
the suitcase,
a silent witness
with two labels

"Masaryk Station, Praha"
"Royal Scot, London – Glasgow"

Leather suitcase
from a far-off country,
Czechoslovakia,
containing all the love
parents could pack
for a five year old
off on a journey
for life.

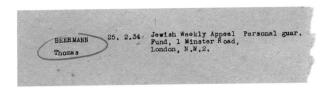

Karel Reisz
**World-renowned
Film Director
Great Britain**

I was born in 1926 in the town of Moravská Ostrava. My memories of Czech schools are very happy ones. We had an excellent drama club and a very friendly headmaster, who was also very active in the Czechoslovak Broadcasting Company. It was a very enjoyable time.

When the political situation became more critical, my mother insisted that we explore all possibilities for our entire family to emigrate. My father resisted, however, because he knew that he would be unable to obtain exit permits for us all. But he had hope that

Karel Reisz's parents

it would at least be possible for me, because in the spring of 1939, he had heard about the children's transports. One day, my father had an argument with his German colleague, who was a Nazi, and soon after this the Gestapo arrested him.

Nonetheless, I was still scheduled to depart on the children's transport. Before my departure, my mother sent me to my Uncle Sigmund, who was a

dentist. She told him to remove all my fillings and replace them with the family gold. Afraid that I would encounter hard times in England, she thought I would need money, and she knew this was one way the family gold would never be found by the Nazis!

My mother accompanied me to the railway station, and I departed convinced that my parents would soon follow. I never saw them again. After the war, I returned to Ostrava and discovered that none of my family had survived the war. I immediately returned to England, where I remained indefinitely.

I very much wanted to get into the film industry, but I didn't know how. How could I join those happy, but mysterious people who make films? How could I become one of them?

I was fortunate. By sheer chance, I was asked to write a book about film editing.

Subsequently, I became a film critic and wrote for an avant-garde film magazine. From there it was only

a short step to directing documentaries and feature films.

Karel Reisz was one of the founders of the new wave in British filmmaking. He directed *Saturday Night and Sunday Morning* (1960), and later *The French Lieutenant's Woman* (1981), which was his most

famous film, starring Meryl Streep and Jeremy Irons. In 1990, he directed *Everybody Wins*, based on the

Karel Reisz with Meryl Streep during the filming
of The French Lieutenant's Woman, *1981*

work of Arthur Miller, starring Nick Nolte. Sadly,
Karel Reisz died in November 2002 in London.

REISZ   21. 7.26   Miss H. Bennett,   Deposit
Karel   415 Addison House,
                        Grove End Rd.N.W.8.

Amos Ben Ron
Engineer
Israel

I was born in April 1930, in Prague. My mother,
Hilde, was a famous violinist. She played at concerts
and, before she married, had toured all of Central
Europe, Austria, Germany, and Italy.

My name then was Peter Brunner, and I managed to get to England with my brother, Tommy. I still remember that on June 30, 1939, our entire family came to the train station to see us off. There was my grandfather and grandmother and Aunt Vilma with her children. It was not until we boarded the train that it sank in that we were really leaving.

We left Prague shortly after midnight. We crossed all of Germany without a hitch; but just before we

*Matej Mináč with Amos Ben Ron and his grandchildren
during the filming of the Winton documentary, 2000*

crossed the border into Holland, the train stopped. German soldiers boarded the train and decided to search it. When they entered our compartment, one of the soldiers reached for a small suitcase belonging to a six-year-old boy. He opened the suitcase and turned it upside down, dumping its contents. I must have turned red and my fellow travelers asked me, "What is wrong with you?" "I don't know," I replied. "I just don't feel well."

Then we reached Holland. Once we stopped at a small village, we were all very relieved. The villagers were very friendly and served us hot chocolate and huge cheese sandwiches. They never stopped talking to us, but we did not understand a word they were saying.

After our arrival in London, we waited at the Liverpool Street Station for someone to pick us up. A number of people read the tags hanging from our necks. Ultimately, a small woman arrived and said,

"These are our children." She introduced herself as Eve Molton. She was accompanied by an elderly man who was a Baptist minister from Clacton-on-Sea. He drove us all to our new home.

I treasure a letter written to us by our parents in their broken English for our birthdays in 1941:

"Dear Peter and Dear Tommy!!

We hope this letter will arrive just in time for your birthday. It is the second you celebrate far from us. How would we be pleased to stay with you both!!

But our hearts and our minds are close to you, and you must feel it that we have no more ardent desire, than to join you one day in healthiness and safety. Therefore, be quiet and happy until we shall meet again. There are no words enough to express all our wishes, but, we think, by wishing you—from the bottoms of our hearts—all the best for your Health, Safety, and Happiness we have said all that loving parents may wish."

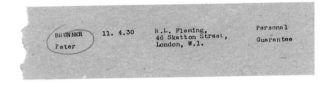

Lord Alfred Dubs
former Parliament Member & Government Minister Great Britain

My most dramatic recollection goes back to 1939, when the Nazis entered Prague. We were forced to tear the picture of Czechoslovak President Edvard Beneš out of our textbooks and insert instead a photograph of Adolf Hitler. It must have symbolized something. I remember the day when Adolf Hitler arrived in the Czech lands and our whole school had to go to the center of Prague to greet him. My mother disagreed with it and prevented me from going, saying that I was too little.

213

My parents must have been very unhappy and anxious when they were preparing me for my trip to Britain. I was too young to understand it all. For me, it was a holiday trip and a tremendous adventure. My mother and her friend took me to the station. I was aware of my mother's nervousness, but I did not understand the reason for it. I remember German soldiers standing on the platform with swastikas on

their uniforms, and that there were a lot of children and grown-ups. The train was late and there was a lot of tension in the air, but this was also something I could not understand.

I was seven years old and spoke two languages because my father was Czech and my mother was Austrian. I was much more fortunate than most other children, because my parents managed to get out of Czechoslovakia and follow me to England. Unfortunately, soon after their arrival, my father tragically died.

I grew up in Manchester, where my mother had found a job. During the last two years of the war, I attended the Czechoslovak boarding school in Wales.

When the war ended, my mother considered returning to Czechoslovakia. She did go back, only to learn that none of our relatives had survived. So, she decided that we would not return.

Alfred Dubs with Nicholas Winton and Milena Greenfell-Baines, another Winton child

THE LOTTERY OF LIFE

Alfred Dubs in the House of Lords

Many years later, I returned to Prague and visited my former home. It was a very strange experience. I stood in front of the house in which I had spent many happy childhood years, but I did not dare to go inside.

I wanted to understand why we had had to flee from the Czech lands, and what Hitler and the Nazis were

Alfred Dubs and other Winton children at the premiere of the film All My Loved Ones *in London in 2000*

really after. Why did the war break out? What was it all about?

I was passionately interested in history and politics at an age when most children have other interests. Already then I decided to become a politician. I said to myself, "If politics are the source of all evil, perhaps they can also be the means through which evil can be avoided."

After the completion of my military service, I studied at and graduated from the London School of Economics. I then joined the British Labor Party, and in 1979 was elected to the British Parliament. Later, I became member of the House of Lords, and after the Labor Party election victory, I became the Minister for Northern Ireland.

Alfred Dubs with Queen Elizabeth II

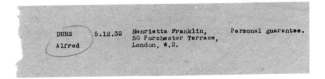

DUBS   5.12.32   Henrietta Franklin,   Personal guarantee.
Alfred   50 Porchester Terrace,
                  London, W.2.

Josef Ginat
Engineer
Israel

My family lived in the Sudetenland region of Czechoslovakia. In 1938, after the Munich Agreement, the situation got so bad that we had to escape. We took only those possessions that we were able to carry. First, we went to Staňkov, then to Beroun, and ultimately ended up in Prague. It was a desperate time. My mother realized that in order to save us, she had to get us out of the country. So, she arranged for our departure and sent us, her four children, away. We left on the last Winton transport in the beginning of August 1939.

In England, I was taken in by a Christian minister who did everything possible to help me retain my Jewish religion. He modified part of his church to

resemble a synagogue, and even obtained a Jewish scroll (Torah) for which his wife embroidered a covering. The minister would say to me, "I pray in my way, so you should pray in your way, according to your tradition and religion."

One day the minister bought me some new clothes, and I was able to wear a new suit for the first time. I was very proud of it! They took a picture of me in my suit, and I felt really important.

After the war, I settled in Israel and worked as an engineer. I married an American woman named Tamara, who had come to help build the new State.

We adopted two children, Elah and Yalon, and we are a very close and happy family.

The Ginats with Nicholas Winton in October 2004

Alice Klímová
(Justitzová)
Teacher
Prague

Like most people, I have had my share of good and bad luck in life. My greatest happiness was my childhood, my parents, my sister Mimka, Grandma, Grandpa, aunts, uncles, and all my cousins. From the day I was born, loving people whom I took for granted surrounded me—until I lost them all.

Alice with her older sister Mimka in 1932

We lived on Bachmačská Street, today called Kafka Street, in the Dejvice area of Prague. My father was a traveling salesman and my mother worked as an administrative assistant in her father's wholesale coffee business. At home, we spoke Czech, but with my grandparents, mostly German. Shortly after my birth, my father became a representative for the Agil Company, a manufacturer of welding electrodes. He started out in a small shop in Strašnice, but when his business grew he moved to Libeň. We lived in a four-room apartment in a villa in the Vinohrady area.

Alice's Father

Although I was very young and had only just begun to attend elementary school, I recall that after the

Munich Agreement of September 1938, my father listened more and more to the news on our new Phillips radio.

I also remember the large number of refugees from the Sudetenland who were crowding the various Prague train stations. Our parents were afraid that war might break out, so they decided to take my sister and me to Czech Sternberg for a week.

On our return home, we ran into my mother's brother and his family, including my cousins Eva and Vera, whom I liked very much.

Only years later did I learn that they had to escape from Dresden, Germany, after the *Kristalnacht* attacks.

On the basis of this photograph, Alice was picked by her English guardians

My sister, Mimka, attended the German high school in Štěpánská Street, while I went to school on Lužická Street. I will never forget March 15, 1939. It was snowing lightly while I was walking to school in the morning. Moravská Street, which runs parallel to Lužická Street, was full of army tanks. Even though I was very young, I realized that something horrible was taking place.

In early June 1939, my parents told me that I would be going to England. Although at the time they had smiles on their faces, only many years later did I realize what a hard decision it must have been for them. I was happy about the trip, because my parents had bought me a whole new wardrobe; up to that

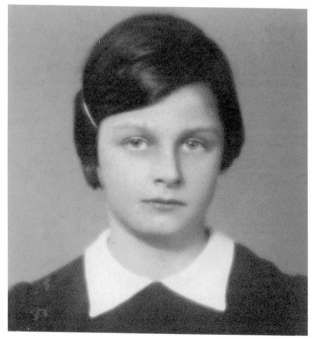

Alice in 1939

time I'd worn only hand-me-down clothes from my older cousins. I was traveling to England in place of my sister, Mimka, because the English foster family wanted a young girl between ten and fourteen years old. As Mimka was already 16, and I only 10, I left Czechoslovakia alone.

At that time, the only way children could get to England was as part of a children's transport. I remember going with my mother to a building on Voršilská Street to be registered for the transport. Only fifty years later did I learn that the apartment served as an office for Nicholas Winton, the organizer of the children's transports. My departure from Masaryk Station in Prague was set for midnight on June 29, 1939. The school year had ended on that day; I had successfully completed my fifth year of primary school.

To celebrate, my sister Mimka had taken me to Ruská Street for Italian ice cream with whipped cream on top.

For my journey, my mother packed a steamer trunk for me, which could not weigh more than 50 kg. I also received a canvas bag full of food from my grandmother, which included fresh apricots. My parents, Mimka, my cousin, as well as friends of our family accompanied me to the station. My parents were smiling and so was I. It was not until the train began to move that I noticed tears in my father's eyes. I cheerfully called out to him, "Daddy, don't spray the platform—you'll embarrass me!"

Although I do not recall much about the journey, I do remember sleeping on the floor of a large room

225

on the ship and seeing two older girls changing the diapers of six-month-old twins. They were the youngest children in the transport. The Dutch people who owned the ship gave us hot chocolate and some strange white bread that I threw out of the porthole. I was not the only one to do so!

On Saturday, July 1, 1939, we arrived at London's Victoria Station. To get us adjusted to life in England, they had organized a camp for a week in Essex. We had a good time, and I celebrated my eleventh birthday there. After that, we went to our individual guardian families. Because my guardians did not yet have a bed for me, I stayed with my friend Lia Wiener and her foster family in a suburb of London. Lia once began crying because she was homesick. I immediately joined in. In that state of mind, both of us wrote letters to our parents telling them how homesick we were. I even wrote that in desperation I might swim across the English Channel to get home. Soon thereafter, letters arrived from my mother, from my aunts, and even my grandmother. They all tried to calm me down. But by the time their letters reached me, I had long forgotten about being homesick.

In the middle of June, John Marshment came to pick me up and took me to my new home.

The place is called Garston and is just outside London. The Marshments had a nice house and gave me a room to myself. I hardly had time to look around before I received a letter from my sister Mimka, telling me that she would be arriving in England on July 20. In fact, her letter reached me

The Marshment family (R. to L., John Sr., Alice's stepbrother John, Olga and Alice) during a visit to Prague in 1963

on the morning of the day that Mimka was due to arrive! In my poor English, I attempted to tell my foster mother, Olga, that my sister was coming.

She dressed her four-month-old baby, and we left immediately by underground subway to meet Mimka. It was my first trip in the underground, and I could not understand why one was not permitted to wear a dinner jacket. My misunderstanding came about because there were "No smoking!" signs everywhere, and "smoking" is the Czech word for "dinner-jacket!"

Mimka arrived on the next children's transport, and the station was packed with prospective guardians who were waiting for the new members of their families. There was chaos and noise everywhere.

We hardly had time to say hello to Mimka before she was taken off by the Aronson family. She was to begin training to be a nurse.

Mimka didn't have an easy life, as she worked long hours and received little food and even less money. I,

227

on the other hand, lived very well. My foster parents even took me to the seaside!

Mimka was now not only my sister, but also my friend, advisor, moral supporter, and when necessary, my mother. She performed all these duties with love and total dedication.

Until May 1940, we corresponded with our parents, first through Holland, then via Brazil, and finally,

Mimka in her nurse's uniform, 1940

until our letters were sent to the ghetto town of Terezin in November 1942, through the International Red Cross. These Red Cross messages were limited to twenty words.

Later, Mimka, as a citizen of an enemy country, lost her job in the hospital. (The so-called Protectorate of Bohemia and Moravia was now part of the German Reich, which was at war with Britain. As former citizens of this area, we were therefore officially considered enemies of Britain!)

Alice in 1940

My foster father, John, was called up into the army and his wife, Olga, was expecting her second child, so I had to leave because they could no longer afford to support me. They arranged for my transfer to a middle-aged childless couple in a place called Barrow-in-Furness. After four months there, I was transferred again, this time into the home of

Deutsches Rotes Kreuz   23. MAI 1942   320782
Präsidium / Auslandsdienst
Berlin SW 61, Blücherplatz 2

ANTRAG
an die *Agence Centrale des Prisonniers de Guerre, Genf*
— Internationales Komitee vom Roten Kreuz —
auf Nachrichtenvermittlung

P.163

REQUÊTE
de la Croix-Rouge Allemande, Présidence, Service Etranger
à l'Agence Centrale des Prisonniers de Guerre, Genève
— Comité International de la Croix-Rouge —
concernant la correspondance

1. Absender   **Ida Justitz**
Expéditeur   **Prag XII., Bunzlauergasse 12**
bittet, an
prie de bien vouloir faire parvenir à

2. Empfänger   **Alice Justitz, c/o Mrs. Abrahams**
Destinataire   **41 Holkers Street**
BARROW in Furness, Lancs. England
folgendes zu übermitteln / *ce qui suit:*
(Höchstzahl 25 Worte!)
(25 mots au plus!)

**Uns geht es allen sehr gut. Herzliche Glück-
wünsche zum Geburtstag, werden Deiner
innigst gedenken. Grüssen und danken
Abrahams. Grüsse Erwin. Tausende Küsse Dir
und Mimi.**

Ida Justitz

(Datum / date)

(Unterschrift Signature)

3. Empfänger antwortet umseitig
Destinataire répond au verso   15 JUIN 1942

The last censored letter from my mother was dated June 1942 the Abrahams family. They were orthodox Jews who had come to England from one of the Baltic countries. At home in Czechoslovakia we hadn't observed Jewish religious rituals, and so their way of life was foreign to me. Nevertheless, I tried very hard to adapt and hoped that all that praying would help save my parents.

The Abrahams did not want me to visit my sister for fear that I might eat food that was not kosher. They finally relented when Mimka wrote that I could live with her neighbor who was a rabbi. Mimka was not happy that I was becoming an orthodox Jew, but she was even more concerned that I was forgetting the Czech language. She arranged for me to go to the Czechoslovak state boarding school, and I joined in March 1942.

The boarding school was in the western part of England. Here, Czech teachers taught Czech and Slovak children, and I loved it. More and more students kept arriving, and, before long, we had outgrown the facility. In September 1943, the new school year began in a new and larger building in Wales. The teachers at the Czechoslovak state boarding school had a difficult task on their hands, because of the big differences in the levels of the various students. Nevertheless, we learned a lot. The boys had a soccer team and we girls played handball and field hockey. We rode bicycles and had a choir, a drama circle, and a library. Twice a month, we published our own newspaper.

During holidays, I visited Mimka, even though she was working in a munitions factory. In March

1945, she married a Czech man, Arnošt, who was in the army. When the war ended, she was among the first to return home. She arrived in Prague on June 5, 1945, and went straight to Terezin to help nurse the sick prisoners who had stayed behind after the camp was liberated. When I returned with the rest of the "children" on August 27, 1945, Mimka and her husband were waiting for me at the Prague airport. Not knowing exactly when I would arrive, they went to the airport every day so as not to miss me. In those days, one had a long walk from the last tram stop in Liboce to Prague-Ruzině airport. I was very fortunate to have Mimka. I didn't have to go to an orphanage like many of the returning children, or to a boarding house like the older ones.

Life wasn't easy. Our parents did not return, and, as a matter of fact, neither did any of our relatives. Mimka was expecting a child, and she and her husband had nowhere to live. Food was rationed, and moreover, they were burdened with me, a constantly hungry seventeen-year-old girl! Finally, Arnošt was able to get a two-room basement apartment into which we

Alice and her husband in 1948

all squeezed: Mimka, her husband, their infant Eva, Arnošt's sister, and I.

Slowly, we started living again. I finished high school. My brother-in-law began to study chemistry at the university, while also working at the State Health Institute. Mimka found a job at the archives of the newspaper *Rudé právo*.

After finishing high school, I attended and graduated from the Pedagogical Faculty of the University and got married. My husband, Bob, worked at the Ministry of International Trade, but in 1951, he was fired when the Communists found that he had served against Hitler in the British Army. With our small son, we were forced to move out of Prague and to the countryside in the border region. Here we spent fifteen rather unhappy years. It was not until 1966, when the political situation improved a little, that we were able to return to Prague.

Although I lost all my relatives, I regularly meet with and write to my schoolmates from the Czech school in Wales. They are now members of my family. Vera Gissing and I are like inseparable sisters.

As so many other "Winton children," I also feel that I owe a debt for having been saved. Thus, I try to make a small contribution by attending *The Power of Good* film showings at Czech Schools, where I can talk to the students. Their interest, many questions, and lovely letters give me great joy.

JUSTITZ 5. 7.28   Woodcraft Folk,   Czech Section
Alice   13 Ritherdon Road,
                   Tooting, S.W.
                   CHARLES SKIN LEATHER, CHEPSTOW,
                   BURLEY IN WHARFEDALE, YORKS.

233

FILMS ABOUT
NICHOLAS WINTON

In 1998, I met my old friend, an outstanding film editor and producer, Patrik Pašš. I shared with him the story of Nicholas Winton, and I mentioned to him that one of the children he rescued is the world-renowned Czech-British movie director, Karel Reisz. Reisz directed the romance, *The French Lieutenant's Woman*, which starred Jeremy Irons and Meryl Streep.

Patrik was taken aback. "Are you serious?" he asked. "Karel Reisz wrote a famous book about film editing, and it was the book that inspired me to become a film editor!"

"So," I replied with a laugh, "If Nicholas Winton

had not rescued Karel Reisz, you would not have become a film editor, and I would not have had such a great colleague as you!"

Patrik wanted to know about Winton's rescue operation down to the very last detail. He was very touched by the story. We both began to wonder what we could do personally to thank Nicholas Winton for what he had achieved. We were troubled by the fact that although he had accomplished so much, the world seemed to have forgotten him. We were aware that Winton was not seeking glory, but all the same it seemed unjust to us that almost hardly anyone knew anything about him. So, we decided to thank him as best we could: we would make a documentary film about him and put our hearts and souls into it.

In the end, we made two films—a feature film and a documentary. This was another surprise to me, but I got used to surprises while working on the Winton project!

Patrik Pašš, Martina Štolbová, and Matej Mináč, with Karel Reisz, during the shooting of the documentary in 2000

235

All My Loved Ones
The Feature Film

The first Winton film, which I directed and Patrik edited, was *All My Loved Ones,* based on the memories of my mother's childhood. As I mentioned earlier, I did not like the original sad ending and decided to weave into the narrative the story of Winton's rescue mission.

The film All My Loved Ones, *is distributed in Europe by Beta Film, a German company.*

The renowned British actor, Rupert Graves, played the part of Nicholas Winton. After the film premiered in 1999, journalists sought Winton's opinion on Graves' performance. "He acted very convincingly," Winton said, "I truly felt as if I had gone back sixty years. But," he added, with a grin, "I was much more handsome in those days." Nicholas Winton could not resist making this witty remark, and the journalists erupted in laughter.

Rupert Graves, in the role of Nicholas Winton, reassuring Sosha that she will leave for England on the next train. Sadly, that train never departed.

The film is a co-production of four countries: the Czech Republic, Slovakia, Poland, and Germany.

Jiří Hubač wrote the screenplay; the producers were Jiří Bartoška and Rudolf Biermann; the cinematographer was Dodo Šimončič; and Polish composer Janusz Stoklosa wrote beautiful music.

Many outstanding actors appear in the film, including Jozef Abrhám, Libuše Šafránková, Jiří Bartoška, Jiří Lábus, Ondřej Vetchý, Tereza Brodská, Květa Fialová, and Marián Labuda. The leading child´s role was played by Braňo Holiček. He played David, the ten-year-old son of Dr. Jakub Silberstein.

The Silberstein family believes in justice and humanity, but they are concerned about what the future may bring. David's world revolves around his friend, Sosha, and his fun-loving uncles.

Libuše Šafránková, Jozef Abrhám, and Braňo Holiček, in the role of David

His father's brother, Samuel, is a world-renowned violinist who loves life and lives it to the fullest. His second loves are drinking, gambling, cigars, and women. Having had his share of affairs, he decides to settle down.

He finds the love of his life and intends to get married. The problem is that his wife-to-be is of another faith, and there is resentment in both their families, which they must try to overcome.

Another of David's father's brothers is Leo, a fervent interpreter of the Jewish Talmud and the living conscience of the family. He is most concerned about their lukewarm regard for the Jewish faith.

Jiří Bartoška played the role of the famous violinist at the side of the renowned Polish actress, Agnieszka Wagner

Marcel, yet another brother, is a somewhat absent-minded scientist and inventor. His inventions serve primarily as entertainment for the family.

David likes his uncle Max the most, as he ran a circus with a merry-go-round and swings until the Nazis expelled him from his home in the Sudeten region.

As the situation in Czechoslovakia becomes more and more critical, many people begin to plan their escape. Thanks to Uncle Samuel, the violin virtuoso, the family meets Nicholas Winton, who is in Prague organizing the children's rescue mission. The encounter enables the family to send David to London, which saves his life. David's friend, Sosha, has no such luck. Due to some bureaucratic error, Sosha does not board David's train. She is scheduled to depart on the next Winton transport, but war breaks out, and Winton's largest transport of 251 children never leaves Prague.

*Nicholas Winton at the October 1999 premiere of the film,
with the lead child actors at his side*

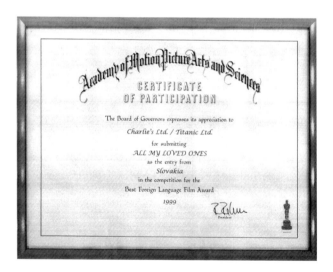

The film was screened at sixty international film festivals. It has won many awards, including:

The Academy Award Motion Pictures Arts & Sciences—Oscar nomination as a foreign film for the Slovak Republic

2000 Festroia: Troia International Film Festival in Setubal Portugal—OCIC Award

2000 International Film Festival, Sedona, AZ, USA—Grand Prix

2000 Annual Czech Film Prize—the "Czech Lion" to Jiří Bartoška for Best Supporting Actor, Czech Republic

Prize of the Slovak Filmmakers' Association, IGRIC 2000

Czech-American Director Ivan Passer, Jiří Bartoška, and the American actor Woody Harrelson after a successful screening at the Karlovy Vary Film Festival

241

AUDIENCE AWARDS:

International Film Festival—Palm Springs, CA, USA—voted by audience as second best of 180 films screened.

Finále Festival—Plzeň, Czech Republic

Washington Jewish Film Festival—Washington DC, USA

Sao Paolo Jewish Film Festival—Sao Paolo, Brazil

Festival of Festivals—Palm Springs, CA, USA

Würzburg Film Festival—Würzburg, Germany

Atlanta Jewish Film Festival—Atlanta, GA, USA

In 2000, the film opened the Czech and Slovak Film Days in London. Of course, the organizers didn't miss the opportunity to invite Mr. Winton, who lives in nearby Maidenhead. When the film ended, Winton appeared on the stage and received a standing ovation. It was a very touching and emotional experience.

The next day, Winton invited me to his home in Maidenhead. After an exhausting schedule of screenings and social activities, I was looking forward to a relaxing afternoon in his pleasant company. How wrong I was! The moment I stepped in the door, Winton told me that he needed a print of the film as soon as possible in order to have a screening in his home town.

Matej Mináč with Nicholas Winton in his garden in 2000

"After all, no one here knows that someone made a movie about me!"

I tried to explain to him that it wasn't so easy to get a copy of the film. The European rights to screen were with the German company Beta Film - München, which also owned the 35mm prints required for screening. I assured Winton that I would try to arrange a screening when I returned to Prague.

"I know such promises," Winton countered. "You will return to Prague and find a thousand different things to take care of. You will forget all about me. Try to make the arrangements right now, from here. There is the phone, so get on with it!" I realized that this was the end of the peaceful afternoon I had hoped for. "But I don't have any of the telephone numbers with me," I protested. "You will find them," he assured me, with a smile on his face.

That was nothing left for it but to start making calls.

I sat down and called Prague; Bratislava in Slovakia; and Munich in Germany. I even called Mallorca, Spain, where, at that time, the person responsible for the film at Beta Film was vacationing. When I finally reached her in her hotel, she gave me her colleague's phone number in Berlin. He in turn referred me to another colleague.

I made calls for four hours until I broke out in a sweat. In the end, however, I was successful and secured a copy of the film for Maidenhead. Winton just smiled and called the cinema immediately to set a date and time for the screening. When I looked at my watch, I realized that I had better hurry up and catch the last train of the day to London.

"What an afternoon," I grumbled as I dropped, exhausted, into a seat on the train back to London. Then I smiled, imagining Nicky Winton in 1939, hounding the officials at the British Home office to issue Entry Permits to Britain for the children, just as he had hounded me that afternoon. I imagined how apprehensive they must have been when they found out that this determined man was heading their way! They eventually realized that the best course of action, in order to get rid of him, was to give in and comply with his requests.

"It is clear to me," I said to myself, "that Winton's fundamental asset is his obstinacy. Whatever he puts his mind to, he is determined to achieve, come what may! He doesn't accept that some things can't be done. This is why he managed to save so many children; he simply made a decision and acted upon it."

NICHOLAS WINTON'S OPINION ABOUT THE FEATURE FILM "ALL MY LOVED ONES"

Dear Matej,

I have been thinking a great deal about the film and thought you and your team might be interested with my reaction to it.

In the past, the films I have seen about the Shoah have in the main been confined to herding people into cattle trucks and marching them down railway lines to the camps.

The agony of those moments has been well and truly documented, but the tensions within the family about the seriousness of the situation, the agony of decision making and the disbelief that the worst could happen, I see for the first time in your film.

The tragedy that it is the goodness of people who cannot believe in utter evil and bestiality, that is well shown.

Greetings Nicky

P.S. You wanted photos of my tapestries – I enclose 2 which are Russian carpet designs.

Nicholas Winton: The Power of Good
The Documentary Film

This is the first film that describes in detail the story of Nicholas Winton's rescue mission about which he remained silent for fifty years.

Thanks to the international success of this documentary, the humanitarian message of the rescue mission is spreading throughout the world.

Janusz Stoklosa composed the music, and the editor was my friend Patrik Pašš, who also co-produced the film with me.

During the gala award ceremony in New York on November 25, 2002, the film won an International

The documentary's production team accepting the International Emmy award

Emmy Award for the best documentary. It was the first time that a Czech or Slovak documentary was so honored.

We assumed that we were attending the prestigious gala ceremony as observers. We did not expect to have even a chance of winning, because we had fierce competition from large TV production companies such as ZDF from Germany, CBC from Canada, NHK from Japan, and the BBC.

In order to attend the award ceremony, I had to purchase a tuxedo, as formal attire was mandatory. Since our chances were very slim, I was not prepared to spend much money. I purchased the cheapest tux I could find. It was made from some synthetic material, and, in hindsight, it turned out to be a wise decision.

The synthetic material was wrinkle-free, and when I appeared on the stage to accept the award, I looked as if I had purchased a very elegant, expensive tuxedo.

My wife, Karin, approached the situation very differently. She was quite convinced, right from the beginning, that we would win; so her only concern was to be dressed in top-notch attire. Every third day she posed in a new dress that she either purchased or borrowed from one of her girlfriends. It appeared to me a total waste of time and money.

"Don't overdo it, we have no chance of winning the award," I said to her, although I have to admit that her new clothes were very becoming. When I was called during the gala to come up with Patrik to accept the award she whispered to me, "What did I tell you? It was clear to me from the very beginning!"

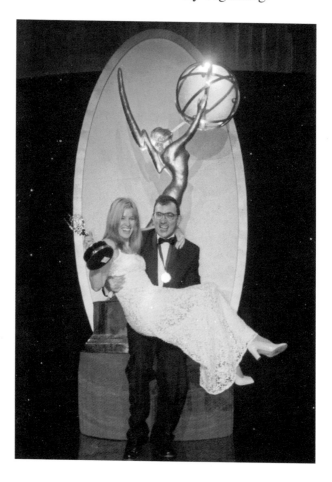

Ever since then I listen to her more than ever and even do not mind her ever-expanding wardrobe. I decided to keep my inexpensive tuxedo for two reasons: first, it brought me luck, and, secondly, because I can be sure that moths will never come near it!

The New York City premiere of the documentary took place on October 18, 2002, in the Symphony Space Theatre on Broadway in New York City. The show was completely sold out. The organizers did not expect to sell all the 1,000 tickets to their regular subscribers, so they decided to make the tickets available to the public through their box office.

Matej Mináč, Patrik Pašš, and Martina Štolbová in New York City, 2002

Wouldn't you know it! *The New York Times* printed a highly complimentary article about the documentary and Mr. Winton. The article also announced that Mr. Winton would attend the premiere. The tickets sold out almost immediately, which caused some problems for the organizers. Eight ambassadors, representing countries where some of the "children" live, confirmed their attendance. Even former U.S. President Bill Clinton and his wife Hillary planned to attend, as did the Mayor of New York City, Michael Bloomberg. But there were no tickets left! So, the only option available to the organizers was to ignore the safety precautions and to place these eminent people in seats that were strictly reserved in case of emergency!

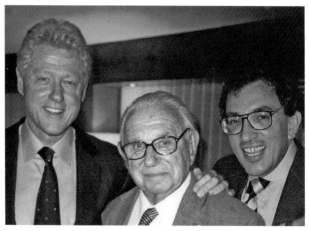

Part of the activities surrounding the New York premiere was a meeting with the former President of the United States, Bill Clinton

I must admit that the huge interest in the documentary was very pleasing. It was a filmmaker's dream come true! The hall was completely sold out, but people still waited outside the cinema hoping in vain that a seat would be found for them.

From around the United States, nineteen Winton "children" came to the New York premiere. Joe Schlesinger, the renowned CBC journalist who narrated the documentary, came from Canada. When he invited Nicholas Winton to the stage at the end of the screening, the standing ovation was endless. It was a fantastic feeling!

We spent an entire week in New York City. Nicholas Winton was interested in everything. He wanted to see the Museum of Modern Art, the Museum of Natural History, and Ground Zero, the site of the terrorist attack against the United States on September 11, 2001.

His planned itinerary was so exhausting that every evening we all fell into our beds completely worn out, while he was as fresh as can be. One evening, when we tried to convince him to turn in a little early and get some sleep, he retorted, "We did not come to New York to rest, did we?" So, off we went into the nighttime streets of New York City.

Nicholas Winton enjoyed himself immensely in New York. He even had a white tuxedo tailored for the occasion

I must share with you another story connected with Nicholas Winton's visit to New York. On a number of occasions Winton told me about the important role the Czechoslovak travel agency Čedok played in his rescue efforts in 1939. They helped him take children out of Czechoslovakia by offering him discounted rail fares. Without this valuable assistance, Winton's rescue mission would have been much more difficult.

That is why, when preparing to work on the documentary about the rescue mission, we turned to JUDr. Jiří Šimaně and Čedok for cooperation. To our delight, they agreed. They became a major partner in the documentary project. Thanks to them, the film was distributed not only to Czech theaters, but also around the world.

Winton has vivid recollections of his collaboration with Čedok

When we were planning our trip to the United States, we were concerned about the toll the long flight would take on Winton, who was 93 years old at the time. The Čedok management did not see a problem. "We will fly him on the supersonic Concorde jet, and he will be in New York in three and a half hours. That will give him hardly enough time to have a cup of coffee and a little rest."

Mr. Winton was thrilled by the offer. "The flight on the Concorde is even more exciting than visiting New York City. It is high time for me to try it. If not now, then when?"

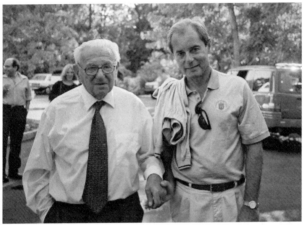

JUDr. Jiří Šimáně with Nicholas Winton in New York

Nicholas Winton's 94th birthday present
– a flight on an ultra-light aircraft

Thus, thanks to Čedok, Winton's dream was fulfilled. He always was crazy about airplanes. As a gift on

253

his 94th birthday, he received a ride on an ultra-light aircraft above his home in Maidenhead. In doing so, he became the oldest person on the planet to fly in such a fragile aircraft!

When the Concorde flights were terminated, Winton called me immediately and said "Matej, wasn't it wise that I took the Concorde to New York? It was really the last opportunity!"

The Certificate of Merit given to Nicholas Winton by the Governor of the State of New York, Mr. George Pataki

The London premiere of the documentary took place in September 2002, at the Barbican Centre. On this occasion, the British Minister for European Affairs, Peter Hain, presented Mr. Winton with a letter from Prime Minister Tony Blair. In the letter, the Prime Minister acknowledged Mr. Winton's efforts and thanked him for all he had done.

The British government recommended to the Queen that Mr. Winton be knighted. Accordingly, Queen

10 DOWNING STREET
LONDON SW1A 2AA

5 September 2002

THE PRIME MINISTER

Dear Mr. Winton,

I am delighted that the documentary film about you is being shown publicly for the first time in Britain. This film is long-overdue recognition of your extraordinary humanitarian achievement in saving hundreds of Czechoslovak children from death.

Your initiative and determination in the months leading to the outbreak of the Second World War remain an inspiration. The selfless commitment you showed, and steadfast will to ask "What can I do to help?", and then to act, are examples to us all. That you did it in the face of seemingly insurmountable odds makes what you did all the more remarkable.

The people you saved, and their children, many thousands together, are a living and heartwarming testament to your courage.

Thank you for all you have done.

Yours sincerely,

Tony Blair

Mr Nicholas Winton

Elizabeth II knighted Nicholas Winton on March 11, 2003, thus making him Sir Nicholas Winton. If I tried to address him as "Sir" in private, however, he probably would give me a clip around the ear! But being knighted did please him. For one thing, it helped him in his charitable activities, because it made it easier for him to raise funds for the construction of a new senior citizens' center called "Winton House" in Windsor.

Once he said to me, "You see, I can't pass away yet, I still have to finish Winton House," with his raw sense of humor that is so typical of him.

255

Today, he is renowned and admired, but from time to time he blames me. "You ruined me, Matej!" he says. "Since your films, I do not have a peaceful moment, and since I became 'Sir,' it is even worse. My home is in constant motion. All the time people ask for interviews, invite me to attend functions, and I receive sacks of mail. I have so much work that I could use four secretaries! Where are those good old days when I had time to dig in my garden and grow vegetables?"

Nicholas Winton in his garden

THE AWARDS WON BY THE DOCUMENTARY:

Winner of the 2002 International Emmy Award for outstanding documentary program —
New York, 2002

Nominee for the 2006 News and Documentary Emmy Award representing HBO/CINEMAX —
New York, 2006

2006 Christopher Award for the film that affirms the highest values of the human spirit —
New York, 2006

Pacific Jewish Film Festival Spirit Award —
USA, 2005

The 19th Troia International Film Festival Special Mention — Portugal, 2002

TRILOBIT Prize Czech Film and Television Association — Czech Republic, 2002

Slovak Film Critic's Prize Club of Slovak Film Journalists SSN — Slovak Republic, 2002

Prize IGRIC Slovak Film Association & Union of Slovak TV creators — Slovakia, 2002

Etnofilm Prize — Slovak Republic, 2002

Prize of the Nine Gates Film Festival — Czech Republic, 2002

Warsaw Jewish Film Festival First Award —
Poland 2002

AUDIENCE AWARDS:

Washington Jewish Film Festival—Washington, DC

Miami Jewish Film Festival—Miami, FL

NOTABLE FILM FESTIVAL APPEARANCES:

2002 International Film Festival Closing Gala Film—Palm Springs, CA

International Film Festival—Vancouver, BC

International Film Festival—Karlovy Vary, Czech Republic

Film Festival—Haifa, Israel

Documentary Film Festival—Leipzig, Germany

Jewish Film Festival—San Diego, CA

Jewish Film Festival—Palm Beach, FL

Jewish Film Festival—St. Louis, MO

Jewish Film Festival—Phoenix, AZ

Barbican Film Season—London, UK

On **CinemaNet Europe**, the film was selected as the inaugural film of the first satellite broadcast digital project in 200 cinemas in seven European countries.

EPILOGUE

"Why?"

That is the one-word question people often ask me when I discuss my deep involvement in the Winton story. To keeps things simple, my usual response is, "I was infected by the Winton virus." In reality, however, the reasons for my involvement are much more complex.

I was born in the former Czechoslovakia, where I witnessed a number of tragic events before leaving that country. First, it was the Czechoslovak military mobilizing its forces in anticipation of an attack on its sovereignty by Hitler's war machine. However, an attack did not follow, as Czechoslovakia's allies signed a humiliating agreement with Hitler, which swiftly gave control of my country to the Nazis. This

259

Munich Agreement ceded arbitrarily divided, yet strategically important regions of Czechoslovakia to Hitler in return for his promise not to take military action against the country – a promise he and his armies would not keep. Shortly after the agreement, the Czech lands were occupied by Germany, and the newly created Slovak state became an ally of Nazi Germany. The Nazi occupation was not kind to me, and by the time Czechoslovakia was liberated, and I with it, I was an orphan just a little over twelve years old. My mother was arrested on her 37th birthday. The only thing that remained of her, other than fond memories, was a green overcoat. The brutes who arrested and hauled her away would not permit her to take her overcoat, though the winter weather was at its peak on December 13, 1944. Only a few years later, the Communist takeover of Czechoslovakia prompted me to leave my homeland for freedom and democracy in the U.S.

Although I am not a "Winton child," I do have one thing in common with them: I feel that I must be willing to do some good in the world as a way of repaying society for all the good things that have happened to me. Although the Winton film told me the story of his incredible rescue efforts, it also taught me four important lessons. First of all, one person can make a difference. Secondly, doing good for others is a powerful way of showing thanks. Third, the unselfish story of Sir Nicholas Winton must be brought to the attention of young Americans. Last, but not least, Winton must be honored by the U.S., primarily because our government turned a deaf ear to his pleas for help almost 70 years ago.

Perhaps if the U.S. government had not done so, the 250 children scheduled to depart from Prague in September 1939 could be counted today among the surviving "Winton children." Instead, they all perished.

Although I am very pleased that I played a tiny role in having President George W. Bush write a letter to Sir Nicholas, I pledge to continue my efforts toward a Congressional recognition of him, and to spread the word of his deeds, heroism, and modesty as long as I am physically able to do so.

Peter A. Rafaeli
Philadelphia, PA
November 27, 2006

SIR NICHOLAS WINTON'S MEMORABLE AND EMOTIONAL VISIT TO PRAGUE

CO-ORGANIZED BY AMERICAN FRIENDS OF THE CZECH REPUBLIC

From October 6-12, 2007, Sir Nicholas Winton, accompanied by his daughter, Barbara, and son, Nick, visited Prague at the invitation of H.E. Karel Schwarzenberg, Minister of Foreign Affairs, and Mr. Václav Havel, former President of the Czech Republic. Sir Nicholas attended Forum 2000 as the event's sole guest of honor. Following Forum 2000, Sir Nicholas visited the Lord Mayor of Prague, the Hon. MUDr. Pavel Bém.

On Monday, October 8, Sir Nicholas attended the opening ceremony of Forum 2000 and later lunched with H.E. Craig Stapleton, U.S. Ambassador to France and former Ambassador to the Czech Republic. That afternoon, the Czech Minister of Defense, Mrs. Vlasta Parkanová, awarded Sir Nicholas the highest Czech military honor. She thanked Sir Nicholas for saving 669 children, including the mother of one of her top advisors. H.E. Linda Duffield, Ambassador of the U.K., also attended the ceremony with her defense attaché.

On Tuesday, October 9, Sir Nicholas was honored at an auspicious event arranged by Mr. Matej Mináč, creator of the feature film, *All My Loved Ones,* and the highly acclaimed, International Emmy award-winning documentary, *Nicholas Winton: The Power of Good.* A crowd of over 3,000 people, including 2,700 school children, packed the Prague Congress

Center for the two-hour event. The program included performances by two orchestras and a large children's choir who at one point serenaded Sir Nicholas with a piece specially composed for the event. AFoCR was asked to explain to the audience its activities in the U.S. that led to a special letter written by President Bush to Sir Nicholas in July 2006, passage of H.R. 583 by the U.S. House of

L to R: Sir Nicholas, H.E. Linda Duffield, British Ambassador, British Defense Attache, Defense Minister Parkanova, Czech military aide, Jan Soucek, son of Winton child, Mrs. Souckova (speaking)

Representatives, and publication of the educational book by Matej Mináč, *Nicholas Winton's Lottery of Life,* translated from the Czech by Peter A. Rafaeli and published by AFoCR. Provided free of charge to educational institutions nationwide, 17,000 copies of the book will soon be distributed. The Congress Center event was televised by Czech Television nationwide.

*Sir Nicholas escorted into Kongress Centrum Prague
by H.E. Karel Schwarzenberg, Foreign Minister*

Because AFoCR and the Czech Embassy in Washington informed the Office of the President in advance of Winton's upcoming visit, and audience with him was arranged and on Wednesday, October 10, Sir Nicholas, accompanied by his son, Nick, daughter, Barbara, and AFoCR's Peter A. Rafaeli, met with him.

*M.C. Zdenek Tulis asks questions about Winton related
activities in the U.S. and Peter A Rafaeli provides details*

Wednesday's program continued with a luncheon hosted by H.E. Excellency Linda Duffield, the British Ambassador to the Czech Republic. The luncheon was also attended some of the "Winton children," Matej Mináč, and AFoCR's Peter A. Rafaeli. That evening, several of Winton's children also attended a dinner hosted by the Grand Hotel Bohemia. On that day, Peter Rafaeli went to a newsstand asking to purchase those Czech papers that had articles about Sir Nicholas' visit to Prague. The vendor politely suggested that he buy all major Czech newspapers, since all of them covered the visit.

Sir Nicholas Winton with President Václav Klaus

Thursday, October 11, was the "American Day" of the program. H.E. Richard Graber, U.S. Ambassador to the Czech Republic, hosted a reception at the Ambassador's residence. Ambassador Graber presented an original of H.R. 583 passed by the U.S. House of Representatives. The Ambassador

Presentation of PA Senate Congratulatory Message
and copies of U.S. edition of AFoCR book

also read and delivered a letter from Congressman
Ron Klein (FL), the lead sponsor of H.R. 583.
Following the Ambassador's remarks, Peter A.
Rafaeli was asked by Ambassador Graber to present
a congratulatory proclamation issued by the Senate
of the Commonwealth of PA and also the copies of

U.S. Ambassador to Prague, H.E. Richard Graber,
welcomes to his residence H.E. Petr Kolář,
Czech Ambassador to the U.S.

the U.S. edition of *Nicholas Winton's Lottery of Life* by Matej Mináč and translated by Peter A. Rafaeli.

It was indeed a remarkable and highly emotional week. Sir Nicholas Winton deserves it and enjoyed it all. AFoCR is proud to have accomplished this much by bringing the Nicholas Winton Educational Program to the American public and primarily to young Americans.

During this visit Nicky was showered with love, admiration and honors. The Czech population, young, old and anywhere in between, was in an awe about

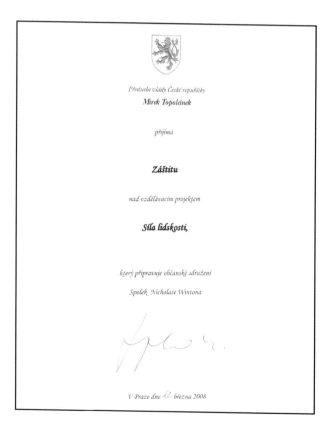

this man who saved 669 of their fellow citizens in 1938-39. After Nicky returned home in fall of 2007 his name was still mentioned in admiration and respect for him. This feeling reached the highest levels of the Czech Government reaching its peak when in March 2008 the Czech Prime Minister, Mr. Mirek Topolánek, gave his auspices to the Nicholas Winton Educational Project.

For further information please contact Peter A. Rafaeli by e-mail to Philadelphia@honorary.mzv.cz or by telephone to 215.646.7777.

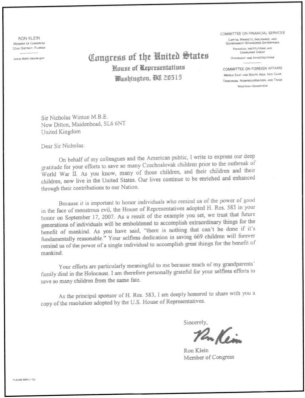

Recognition letter from U.S. Congressman Ron Klein (FL)

THE LOTTERY OF LIFE EDUCATIONAL PROJECT

Everyone is aware of the great pressure placed on American teachers to ensure that their students master educational standards and do well on standardized tests. Yet not a single state expects students to recognize the name "Nicholas Winton." Students aren't required to know the information contained in this book in order to pass a test; but the story of Nicholas Winton's heroic deed is a necessary lesson in ethical living for students and adults, alike. Fortunately, both *The Lottery of Life* and the documentary film *Nicholas Winton: The Power of Good* teach lessons in history, literature, and ethics, and encourage students to think critically about the world around them. *The Lottery of Life* Educational

Project not only helps students meet educational standards and perform well on standardized tests, it also motivates students to become active citizens by teaching the difference one person can make.

THE BOOK'S CONTEXT:

Nicholas Winton's heroic deed occurred in late 1930s Czechoslovakia. As the book explains, depression raged throughout the world during the late 1930s. Many people did not know where they would get their next meal. Unlike so many, Winton had a great job. "The world was his oyster," says narrator Joe Schlesinger in *The Power of Good*. He risked everything to save people he did not know, at a time when he had much. Many states expect students to understand the depression of the 1930s in order to succeed on standardized assessments. This book sheds an interesting light on the Depression.

Numerous states also expect students to develop an understanding of the Holocaust. The *Lottery of Life* does not depict the horrendous gas chambers at Auschwitz, nor does it speak of cramped cattle cars. Instead, it discusses something far more important – the power that a single individual can have in promoting good throughout the world. Literature standards throughout the United States expect students to understand heroism. This book documents a real heroic effort.

Teachers can explicitly connect a reading of this book to state educational standards. Ask students to select three to five standards that reading this book can help them master. Students might develop an argument explaining the validity of their list.

Successfully completing this activity will ensure that they have indeed mastered a number of standards.

ASKING QUESTIONS:

As educators, we don't have to provide our students with all the answers. Rather, we should offer them the contexts to ask their own insightful questions. Curiosity should push students to develop their own answers to these questions, based on evidence and logic. *Nicholas Winton: The Power of Good* provides such a context.

ENGAGING WITH THE IDEAS OF THE TEXT:

Students' desire to participate in their own learning rises when educators use motivating pedagogical strategies to engage the class with a text. Developing dramatic presentations will help students think deeply about the ideas in this book. For example, we know that Joe Schlesinger, his brother and father spent their last night together in a smelly bathroom in the German Reich. What do your students think they did or could have said to one another? Encourage your students to develop skits through which they demonstrate the behavior of Schlesinger's father. They might incorporate the father's thoughts, not just his words. We also know that the Nazi commandant spat in the face of Vera Gissing's father. Students can develop skits as if they were the thoughts in the commandant's, Vera's and her father's heads. What kinds of conversations did Nicholas Winton have with the parents of the children whom he saved? Allow your students to develop creative skits and not only will they read the book, they'll become part of it.

Despite the fact that Mináč wrote this book for middle and high school students, arts and crafts activities can help younger students engage with the text. Provide students with multi-colored construction paper and glue. Tell them that they may not cut or write/draw in this activity. They can only tear and glue. (This eliminates competitiveness.) Now ask students to develop images depicting situations from the book. For example, ask students to depict what a parent's heart might have looked like as

their children departed. What would the child's heart have looked like as s/he departed on the train? What about a foster parent's heart as they awaited the child's arrival in England? After students create their images, invite them to explain why they made them as they did.

THE AUTHOR'S INTENT:

Why did Matej Mináč write this book? He's clearly a very talented producer, director, and writer. What was it about this story that might have captured Mináč's attention? He devoted more than a year of his life to producing the documentary film *Nicholas Winton: The Power of Good* and this book. What's so compelling about this story?

For every page that Mr. Mináč included in this text, he easily could have substituted it with details about another incident related to the rescue or later lives of the children whom Winton saved. Ask your students to consider why the author selected some stories over others. Encourage them to hypothesize as to the type of material that he left out. Instead of introducing numerous children whom Winton saved, he could have limited the story to one or two "children." How would this have altered the author's message?

Encourage your students to get inside of Mináč's head. Empower them to make literary decisions. Urge them to retell the story from their own perspective, their own point of view. Might they change words? What about paragraph structures? How about the order of the chapters?

THE READER'S PERSPECTIVE:

Though it's worthwhile to consider an author's perspectives on a book, it's essential for readers to develop their own perspectives, as well. The first time I read this story, I recognized a central point. To me, the point of this story is that "one" good deed can lead to hundreds of other good deeds. Nobody told me that this was the message that should be taken from it, and others certainly could have taken other lessons. For example, a young mother might deduce that the point is that sometimes a parent has to be willing to let go of her children in order to provide them with the best. Another person may focus on the cruelty of the Nazi regime and perceive this story to be a compelling statement about the depravity of humankind. Although Nicholas Winton saved hundreds of children from certain death by the hands of the Nazis, why did millions and millions of innocent people have to die in the Holocaust?

When we empower our students to read this story as independent-minded readers, they take ownership of the story. Mináč's reasons for writing the story no longer matter. He gave the right to dictate meaning away when he distributed the book. Your opinions and my opinions don't matter, either. Instead, it's our responsibility as educators to push our students to develop their own perspectives of the story. Ask them what the main point of the story is to them. When they read the story, did they have any new realizations that made the experience of reading worthwhile? What one idea from the story do they want to remember for the rest of their lives? Why? Don't let students simply rattle off single sentences. (Judging by students' reactions to the film and book thus far, however, this is hardly the case.) Urge them to look inside of the text to develop arguments that support their answers. Provide students an opportunity to draw one another's attention to different parts of the text that each thinks is meaningful.

CONCLUSION:

No state has educational standards that mandate viewing the documentary film *Nicholas Winton: The Power of Good* or reading the accompanying *Lottery of Life*. Students don't have to know the material in this book, specifically, to pass standardized assessments. They need to know the material in this book, however, to lead meaningful lives. Advantageously, the process of reading and thinking about this book teaches students how to read and analyze textual passages on standardized assessments. *The Lottery of Life* Educational Project helps students excel on standardized tests and in the real world, and inspires them to do good for others and for themselves.

> — Andrew Pass, Educational Consultant
> Bloomfield Hills, MI

TOPICS FOR CLASSROOM DISCUSSIONS

After seeing the documentary film, discussions can be held on a number of topics:

SUBJECT: THE HOLOCAUST

1. Which people were considered by the Nazis to be inferior races? Why do you think the Nazis felt this way?

2. What did the Nazi term, "The Final Solution to the Jewish Question," mean? Why would they refer to the extermination of an entire people in this way?

3. How could the people of a cultured and educated nation such as Germany believe in Hitler's theory of racial superiority? (What was the economic and

historical context for Hitler's rise to power?) Do you think that there are people today that believe their race is superior? In what ways could this belief be dangerous?

4. In what ways is our civil and democratic society different from the one run by the Nazis in Germany?

5. Imagine that, beginning tomorrow, our society will be based on racial superiority. Describe what life would be like.

6. Have you ever felt excluded from your peer group? Have your classmates ever made fun of you? How did you feel? How would you feel if you had to live away from everyone else and had to fear for your own safety and the safety of your loved ones?

7. Do you think that the Holocaust could happen again? Why or why not?

SUBJECT: WHAT IF I WERE IN SUCH A SITUATION?

1. If you were in a situation like the one the children in the film faced, do you think your parents would be able to send you to live with strangers in a foreign land? How would you feel if you had to leave your parents? Would you be excited to travel to a foreign country, as many of Winton's children were?

2. If you, like the children in the film, had to leave for England, what would you pack for the journey?

3. If you were a child in a British family who had adopted a Czech refugee child, how would you feel about your parents becoming foster parents? Imagine receiving only half your allowance and having to

share your room with a stranger. How would you react? Why?

4. How would you feel if you did not know whether your parents were safe? What were the feelings of the children in the film when they returned to Czechoslovakia? Have you ever experienced a situation during which you feared for the lives of your loved ones? Describe the situation.

SUBJECT: PERSONAL RESPONSIBILITY

1. Do you think that Nicholas Winton's deed could be repeated today? Would a strong organization, such as the Red Cross, be beneficial, or do you believe that a group of passionate volunteers would be enough to get the job done? What is the problem plaguing your town, your country, or the world that you would most like to solve? What specific actions could you take to solve this problem?

2. In what ways, if any, are you responsible for people around you who suddenly find themselves in

a difficult situation? Why are you responsible or not responsible? Can you recall a specific instance when you have helped a stranger? If you yourself got into a difficult situation, who would come to help you?

3. Were Nicholas Winton's actions heroic even though his life was not in danger? Why or why not?

SUBJECT FOR AN ESSAY:

1. Imagine yourself as one of the children in the film. Tomorrow, you are to leave for England and bid a final goodbye to your parents. How would you feel? What will happen the day you leave for England?

COMMENTS ABOUT THE FILM

COMMENTS FROM TEACHERS IN THE US AFTER
SEEING THE FILM NICHOLAS WINTON: THE POWER
OF GOOD

"The film's message is literally beyond words. Nicholas Winton is a remarkable human being who models the very best in humanity. The audience was stunned and awed by the experience of watching this film."
— Alan B.

"I will share this inspiring work with my students and urge them to seek truth and act for justice every moment of their lives. Your work deeply affected me, and I will honor your gift for the rest of my teaching life."
— Diane B.

"It is inspiring to see a different aspect of the Holocaust. So often the main focus is on the horrible side, which is important, but equally important is the knowledge that others cared. We are all capable of making a difference."
—Cheryl L.

"The movie is incredible and one that will no doubt impact the lives of students in my classroom. I look forward to sharing it and using the study guide."
—Linda M.

"As a parent, I thought about what it would be like to board my children on a train, knowing I would never see them. What a gift of love!"
—Suzanne M.

"My class at college watched the film on Nicholas Winton. It was powerful. Thank you for sharing this man's story with our group. I teach Social Studies in a small middle school in rural Maine. While viewing the film in the classroom with at least 20 other adults, the room was silent. All of us thought the subject was spell-binding."
—Janice R.

"I will plan on showing *The Power of Good* to my 11th grade US History classes and to my Civil Rights team. Sometimes it is more powerful to show the good of the Holocaust instead of the bad."
—Lindsay H.

"I found the movie extremely moving. I felt like I was one of the parents sending my children to safety. Mr. Winton's story is one I will never forget and I am looking forward to sharing

it with my students. Thank you for adding a powerful tool to my teaching of the Holocaust."
— Margi T.

"I teach a class called 'World At War' at Lakeview High School. This class is an elective class taken by mostly juniors and seniors with the occasional sophomore. We focus on the geopolitical conflicts of the 20th century; however, the class has turned into much more than that.

"One of the stories I share is that of Nicholas Winton by screening the film *Nicholas Winton: The Power of Good*. The story is of a young man with no cares in the world; who came upon an injustice, and simply acted. My students were clearly moved by the power of good that pervaded from the life of Nicholas Winton. While the story is historical, the film can be shared in many different classes, at many different

levels, to children from many different backgrounds — and well it should! The lessons learned are too important not to share. Every teacher should want to show this film to his or her classes, for it shows that even within the context of the Holocaust, hope can live and goodness can flourish.

"Even six weeks after we watched the film, students still commented on Nicholas Winton. I recently asked them to describe Winton in one word, the answers included: 'honorable,' 'courageous,' 'selfless,' and 'inspiring.' His story will live on with them and will, no doubt, affect them in the years to come."

—Scott D.

"I teach in a private high school on the Big Island of Hawaii. Our students are from small islands in Micronesia. For many of them, this is their first time away from their isolated homes. They are all boarded here and for everyone English is a second, third, or fourth language.

"Their background in European history was very limited before coming to our school. To introduce WWII to a sophomore US History course, we studied a brief history of the war in Europe and then watched the film, *Nicholas Winton: The Power of Good*. It served as an outstanding overview of the events leading up to the war, and the story kept these students engaged. The educational experience was extraordinary.

"Our school's motto is: 'Today's students, Tomorrow's leaders,' and this film illustrated what leadership means. After wiping away some tears, our students were excited to do something, even though their relative isolation pulls them farther from world conflicts even than many Americans. They were touched by the film and in their responses noted that one doesn't have to tote a gun, be the president, or make lots of money to make huge and heroic contributions. This experience brought the horrors and hopes of WWII to life for them.

"Thank you for your efforts. This project, like Winton's, is another one of those simple acts that can have profound effects on our world!"
— Michael F.

COMMENTS FROM STUDENTS AFTER SEEING THE FILM NICHOLAS WINTON: THE POWER OF GOOD

"After watching this film, it is incredibly difficult to put to words what I am feeling. This film, course, and readings that I have done over the past few months have been an entirely new education. The kindness and good will of people during such a dark and terrible chapter in world history amazes me. Who could imagine that a gentleman in England could one day touch the lives of thousands of people?

"Your quest to spread the story and educate people is very admirable. The images I saw this evening tore at my heart and emotions. I could never fathom the impact that one person can make on the world.

"Seeing pictures of children separated from their parents forevermore is so moving, and knowing that the deeds of one man can be so powerful is inspiring. This is such an important story that should be told and shown to generation after generation. I wish that there were more I could tell you, but I truly am overcome by and with emotion.

"Thank you very much for sharing with me this wonderful story. I am very grateful."
— Daniel C.

From the author: I was very impressed when I read the letters to Nicholas Winton from 11-year-old boys and girls from one small school in New Jersey. Most of these children had never even heard of the Holocaust, but they all had a wish to do something to help our troubled world. I think these children can teach us adults a lesson or two.
— MM

Dear Sir Nicholas Winton, "I am a student from Mrs. M's reading class and my name is Bobby. I think you are a great role model. It must have taken a lot of guts to do that. I can't believe you saved over 600 kids. I think you are a brave, great man. If I was one of those kids you saved I would be forever grateful. I know you probably heard this a lot, but thank you for saving all of those kids."
Sincerely, Bobby

"I think you are an amazing man. You must be very proud of yourself. I wish I could meet you and find out more about you. I want to do something amazing like you did. A couple of years ago I donated some of my own money to a children's hospital. I always wanted to go to a homeless shelter on Thanksgiving and serve food. I wanted to do that because when I went to [New York City] I saw homeless people on the street. It really made me upset to see them living in boxes. Having a home makes me feel spoiled. I just want to give them some stuff that I have. Thanks for inspiring me to be a better person and do the right thing."

Love, Devin

"How are you? I am really proud of you and want to thank you for everything that you have done. My name is Agnes and I am twelve years old. I love children and have a one-year-old sister. I change, feed and play with her everyday. Now I am looking for a babysitting job. When I grow up I want to adopt all the children in the world so no harm can be done to them. I love you and your amazing work. You really are my hero."

Love always, Agnes

"I just want to say thank you for saving all of those lives. When I watched the movie about you I cried. I can't believe that you had that much courage to do something like that. Thanks to you, Czechoslovakians can remember who saved their lives. My name is Samantha and I am German. I can't believe that those Nazis would even want to do something so terrible...Do you ever wish that you could have done something to stop Hitler?

I do. I wish there were no wars. Remember all those people owe their lives to you. That's special."

Love, Samantha

"Hello, I am Thomas, a student [in New Jersey]. I just want you to know how thankful I am that you saved so many Jewish children. When my teacher first told me about you, I wasn't too interested. But after seeing the movie I became very interested. I don't think even if I tried my hardest I could save 669 kids. How did you feel when you got those kids safely across the sea? How did you feel at the talk show when you saw all the people you saved sitting around you?"

Sincerely, Tommy

"My name is Cory and I just learned about how you saved all those children from being killed. It was amazing what you did. Why didn't you tell anyone about what you did? I am not saying to brag or anything, but just to let people know what a good deed you did. Did you really forget what you did for all those children? At the television show did you know that those people were sitting by you? I am glad you saved so many and I want you to know that I am your number one fan."

Sincerely, Cory

"Hi, I am a sixth grade student [in New Jersey]. I never heard of you before I saw the movie. Let me tell you, Mr. Winton, you are a brave man. I don't know how you did it. I don't know how anyone could be so compassionate. You are and for that I admire you. It was so amazing that you saved all those kids from Prague. Even though they went through the hardship of losing their parents, without you they would have died. All I want to say is thank you. Keep well."

Love, Jordan

"You are a brave man. Did you know the consequences if you were caught? If you saved 669 children, could you imagine what a whole country could have done?… You are my role model and I know I am not the only one who feels this way. Why did you keep it a secret for so long? What you did was the most spectacular, unselfish, kindest thing someone could ever do."

Sincerely, Micaela

"I liked what you did for the children. I think you are a nice man. I want to be like you one day and do something nice for someone. You and I can make a difference if we just chip in and help. You did more than I did and I thank you."

Sincerely, Jeremy

"Hello my name is Kevin. I recently watched a movie about your courageous acts of heroism. I am from a small town in New Jersey. I too want to do something to protect my country and people. When I grow older I want to me a U.S. Marine just like my father. I have always dreamed of helping people just like my father and of course, you. My dad is a police officer and has always wanted to help people. My great grandfather was a U.S. soldier and he always reminded me how the Nazis were bad people and did many bad things. My mom's father was a U.S. soldier during WWII too. All the men in my family were basically in the military. Not all people were bad during the bad times; some prevailed and did good things. You, Mr. Winton, are one of those few people who did their best to make things better, not to destroy. Destroying things, I have learned, is easy, but making things better is hard."

Sincerely, Kevin

"Many questions are running through my mind right now. I really admire what you did for those children. I have a couple of questions. How did you make all those passports? How did you convince all the parents that you were going to take care of their children? Did you ever visit Czechoslovakia before you saved those children? I am really sorry to throw all these questions at you but I am just so interested in this. Learning about you has inspired me to try to help people and do what is right. I am sure that all

those children you saved are very proud of you. I am so glad to have learned about you and I do not think I can thank you enough for inspiring me. Thank you!"
Sincerely, Shaimaa

"Hi, this is Tara. I believe what you did was courageous and brave. We need more people like you in the world. I am not Jewish, but I still appreciate your kindness and decency. I am eleven years old and am obsessed with soccer. I will be representing America when I go to Austria, Germany, and Italy. I also will be working with little kids. You are so modest about what you did. How did you not tell anyone about it? You deserve the appreciation. I want to thank you from the bottom of my heart for saving those children. You changed the world forever."
Sincerely, Tara

"I think what you did was wonderful. Do you have any childhood memories you would like to tell us? Please write us back because I love getting mail."
Sincerely, Kyle

"You are an inspiration to people all over the world. It is amazing how one act of kindness can change the world. You are a brave, kindhearted man. Watching the documentary made me realize how kind people could be. How does it feel to know that because of you 669 children did not die in concentration camps? You are very humble for not telling anyone for so long, but I am glad you finally did. Thank you."
Always, Samantha

"I just watched a video about all that great things that you have done. It's amazing that you transported so many children to England. You knew that if you left the children with their parents they would die. Every time I think of you and what you did, I feel like crying because I know that you were the only thing that stood between those poor children and death. I am part Czechoslovakian. I hope that you will write back soon."

Sincerely, Kate

"Wow! I cannot believe that you were so brave. You made me realize that you shouldn't care so much about yourself, but about the people around you. I just want to say thank you for every single life you saved during WWII. You are an extremely kind man."

Sincerely, Lindsay

"I greatly appreciate what you have done. Being a Jewish boy myself, I am extremely grateful. You didn't have to do it, but you saved 669 on your own. It took a lot of courage to venture out with all those children. You could have been killed! It takes a noble man to do what you did. You have helped the world."

Fondly, Robert

"I watched a movie about you in school. I never knew that it was possible to save so many people. 669 people are more than I know! If I was as brave as you back then, I would have done the same thing, or at least tried to. When my teacher first mentioned what you did I didn't believe it. When we watched the movie I was amazed. It has to be one of the best stories I have ever heard of."

Your fan, Ryan

"I'd like to thank you for saving the lives of all those kids in Czechoslovakia. I think it was a very brave and nice thing you did for people you don't even know and will probably not meet in your life. If it weren't for you, there would be 669 less people in the world, so thank you."

Sincerely, Icaro

"Hello, my name is Anthony. First, I would like to thank you for saving all those children. Why did you put your life on the line for all of them? How did you make this decision? Was it made lightly? Thank you for reading this letter, Sir Winton. I would be extraordinarily glad if you could answer back."

Regards, Anthony

"I was amazed to hear that you risked your life to save 669 children. Mrs. M talks about you as if you are her hero, so that makes me excited to learn about you."

Regards, Kayla

COMMENTS FROM OTHERS AFTER SEEING THE FILM NICHOLAS WINTON: THE POWER OF GOOD

"Thank you so much for the DVD and study guide entitled *Nicholas Winton: The Power of Good*. I just finished watching it at home to see how I can use it with my STARS (Students Taking a Right Stand) Club, which meets every week at Norup School in the Berkley School District. We are going to do a unit on the Holocaust during the month of March. I was so moved by the story of Mr. Winton about the hundreds of Jewish Czechoslovakian children that he saved from the Nazi death camps. My heart is full of hope and pain, and I look forward to sharing parts of this powerful DVD with my club members, who are 5th through 8th graders. My message is always to my students that they must stand up and speak out to make a difference in this world; that if hate goes unchecked, it can turn into genocide. The most beautiful words in this film are when one of the children that he saved speaks about Nicholas Winton's 'common human decency.' That is something that we must teach our children, as they too easily learn about hate."

—Gail K.

"After the War, Nicholas Winton did not publicize his efforts in saving 669 children. The only reason

the world is now learning about this incredible human being is that his wife found an old scrapbook in the attic of their home. In it were the names of all the children he saved along with pictures of many of them. Now in his 90s and in great spirits, Mr. Winton lives in England and has been honored by Kings and Queens. He was not wealthy in 1938. He did not have many connections. He was not super-human. He simply saw a need to do something and he did it with urgency. The descendants of the 669 children Nicholas Winton saved now number over 5,000.

How much more could each of us accomplish if we simply identified something that was important to us and went after it with passion? Perhaps one day there could be many reasons why people should know about your life. If you ever have the opportunity to see the films *Nicholas Winton: The Power of Good* and *All My Loved Ones,* do so. They are profound."

—Boaz Rauchwerger,
Motivational Speaker

"At the 53rd Annual Meeting of the American Academy of Child and Adolescent Psychiatry, October 24, 2006, we presented the Catcher in the Rye Humanitarian Award of the Year to Sir Nicholas Winton.

"The presentation included an excerpt from the film *Nicholas Winton: The Power of Good.* Three individuals who were on the Winton's transport in 1939 and a daughter and granddaughter accepted the award in Sir Nicholas' place.

"The audience of about 1,500 people was deeply moved, gave a standing ovation, and wiped the tears from their eyes. The two-hour program closed with all singing Ode to Joy from Beethoven Choral 9th Symphony and again wiping tears from their eyes."

—Dr. David W. Cline

GLOSSARY OF TERMS

Anschluss: The German word meaning, literally, "connection," but also "annexation," in terms of a political union. "Anschluss Österreichs" is the German phrase for the annexation of Austria into Germany on March 13, 1938.

Anti-Semitism: The hatred or persecution of Jews.

Auschwitz: The German name for the Polish town, Oswietim, located in southern Poland near the Czech border. "Auschwitz" also refers loosely to the three main Nazi German concentration camps and nearly 50 sub-camps built in and near Oswietim, then annexed by and part of Nazi Germany. In June 1940, the Nazis opened their largest concentration camp, Auschwitz I. By 1942, they had also built an extermination camp, Auschwitz II (also called

"Birkenau") where gas chambers operated almost constantly for three years, until Allied armies liberated the camp in April 1945. The site also housed Auschwitz III, (also called "Monowitz") a labor camp. Between 1.1 million and 1.6 million people died in Auschwitz.

Bergen-Belsen: A Nazi prisoner-of-war and transit camp, established in 1943 in the Lower Saxony region of Germany. Never given formal concentration camp status, Bergen-Belsen, under the command of SS-Hauptsturmführer Josef Kramer, became an informal concentration camp, where prisoners who were too weak to work at other camps came to die. The camp was originally built for only 10,000 prisoners, and overcrowding, scarcity of food and shelter, and disease were the main causes of death for the over 30,000 people – including Margot and Anne Frank – who died in Bergen-Belsen. In the last weeks of the war, before British troops liberated the camp in April 1945, the Nazis marched more than 100,000 prisoners to Bergen-Belsen and abandoned them to die.

Buchenwald: One of the first and largest Nazi concentration camps, established in 1937 on a wooded hill in the Upper Saxony region of Germany. ("Buchenwald" is German for "beech forest.") The camp was only open to men until 1944, and many of its 20,000 prisoners worked as slave laborers in nearby factories. In November 1938, 10,000 Jews arrested during and after Kristallnacht were imprisoned at Buchenwald.

Concentration Camp: A large detention center

created for political opponents, prisoners of war, enemy aliens, certain ethnic or religious groups of people, or civilians of a critical war-zone. Concentration camps house prisoners selected according to some criteria, rather than those who are incarcerated after due process of law.

Evian Conference: A conference held from July 6 to July 15, 1938 in Évian-les-Bains, France, to discuss the plight of Jewish refugees from Nazi Germany. Convened at the initiative of US President Franklin D. Roosevelt, delegates from 32 countries attended. However, the conference was unable to pass a resolution condemning the Nazis' treatment of Jews, which further emboldened Hitler and his plans for the extermination of the Jewish people.

Hauptsturmführer: A mid-grade rank in the Nazi SS (abbreviation of "Schutzstaffel," meaning, "Protective Squadron" in German; initially formed in 1925 as Hitler's personal bodyguard, the SS grew to be the unit that perpetrated and supervised the arrest, internment, and execution of Jews and other racial and political enemies of the Nazis). Hauptsturmführer was the most commonly held rank during World War II. Dr. Josef Mengele, who performed inhumane experiments on prisoners at Auschwitz, held the rank of Hauptsturmführer.

Holocaust: A term derived from Greek words meaning "completely" ("holos") and "burned sacrificial offering" ("kaustos"), referring most often to the systematic and state-sponsored and directed persecution of five to seven million European Jews by the Nazi German government during World War

II. The Nazi party believed that ethnic Germans were racially superior and that Jews were racially inferior, "life unworthy of life." After the Nazis came to power in Germany in January 1933, they began persecuting other groups because of their ostensible racial inferiority, including "Roma" (Gypsies), the handicapped, and some Slavic peoples (Poles, Russians, and others). During the Holocaust, the Nazis persecuted other groups of people on political grounds, including Communists, Socialists, Jehovah's Witnesses, and homosexuals.

Home Secretary: Officially called the Secretary of State for the Home Department, the Home Secretary is the chief United Kingdom government minister responsible for the internal affairs of England and Wales, including matters of immigration and citizenship.

Kindertransport: The effort sponsored by the British organization, the Refugee Children Movement, to move all at-risk children from Nazi Germany and the occupied territories of Austria, Czechoslovakia, and Danzig. Although tens of thousands of Jews were able to leave Germany after the Nazi party came to power in 1933, as time passed, it became increasingly difficult to obtain visas in order to leave the country. In transports beginning one month after the Kristallnacht attacks of November 1938, nearly 10,000 predominantly Jewish children emigrated to Great Britain (England, Scotland, Wales, and Northern Ireland) to stay in foster homes and hostels. A number of the older children joined the British or Australian armed forces when they reached the age of 18 to fight against the Nazis. Transports from

Germany stopped on September 1, 1939, the day the German army invaded Poland; now considered the day World War II began. The last known transport left the Netherlands on May 14, 1940, the day the Dutch army surrendered to Nazi Germany.

Kristallnacht: Meaning, in German, "Night of Crystal," Kristallnacht was a pogrom (an organized and officially encouraged massacre of and attack on Jews; from the Russian words meaning, literally, "like thunder," or more generally, "destruction") that was organized by the German government and took place from November 9 to November 10, 1938 in Germany and Austria. Nazi storm troopers and other anti-Semitic Germans and Austrians killed dozens of Jews, destroyed more than 1,000 synagogues, pillaged Jewish cemeteries, schools, and homes, and destroyed all the Jewish-owned businesses that remained in the Reich (some 7,500 stores). During and after Kristallnacht, nearly 30,000 Jews were arrested and sent to concentration camps. The Nazi German government used the murder of a German diplomat as a pretense for organizing Kristallnacht, hence the euphemistically poetic name for the violent pogrom.

Munich Agreement: An agreement signed in Munich on September 29, 1938 between Adolf Hitler of Germany, Neville Chamberlain of Britain, Édouard Daladier of France, and Benito Mussolini of Italy that granted the cessation of the Sudetenland — a region in western Czechoslovakia, home to many ethnic Germans — to Nazi Germany. The agreement established a timeline for the gradual occupation of the entire Sudetenland region by the beginning of

October 1938, and called for the release of Sudeten German political prisoners held by the Czechoslovak government.

National Socialist German Workers Party (NSDAP, or "Nazi" Party): Originally a coalition of the Right-wing National party and Left-wing Socialist party, the Nazi (an abbreviation taken from the German word "Nationalsozialist" meaning "National Socialist") party became an extreme Right-wing party under Hitler after it was democratically elected to power in 1933. Hitler's view of socialism called for equality only among those who had "German blood," and the loss of citizenship and rights of Jews and other "aliens." In its first program, known as the "Twenty-Five Points," published in February 1920, the Nazi party denounced the Treaty of Versailles and called for a reunification of the German people.

Reich: The German word for "reign" or "empire." The Nazi party believed that the Third Reich, which began when the Nazis came to power in 1933 with Adolf Hitler as Chancellor and Head of State, (The Nazis considered the reign of the Holy Roman Empire to be the First Reich, and that of the Hohenzollern empire from 1871-1919 to be the Second Reich) was the beginning of a 1,000-year period in Germany during which the Nazis believed the Aryan master race would lead the world into a new utopian society. The territory of the Third Reich extended beyond Germany to populations of ethnic Germans in Austria, the Sudetenland, and the territory of Memel, as well as several regions acquired by Nazi Germany during World War II;

parts of occupied Poland, Bohemia, and Moravia were also under the immediate jurisdiction of the Third Reich. When the Nazi party fell from power at the end of World War II in 1945, the Third Reich ended.

Sudetenland: A region of Czechoslovakia, near the western border with Germany and home to many ethnic Germans, that was strategically important to Nazi Germany during World War II. The Munich Agreement of September 1938 called for the annexation of the Sudetenland to Nazi Germany.

Terezin: A town in the former Czechoslovakia (called "Theresienstadt" in German), northwest of Prague, used by the Nazis during World War II as a ghetto and "Polizeigefängnis" (German for "Police Prison"). About 144,000 Jews were sent to Terezin beginning in June 1942. Around 88,000 of them were deported to Auschwitz and other extermination camps, and 33,000 died mostly of the appalling conditions (hunger, stress, and disease, including an epidemic of typhus at the end of the war). There were only 17, 247 survivors in Terezin when the war ended in 1945.

Wagner-Rogers Bill: A bill introduced to US Congress in February 1939 by Senator Robert Wagner and Representative Edith Rogers that proposed to admit 20,000 German refugee children into the United States. The bill never passed into legislation.

SUPPLEMENTARY MATERIAL

Nicholas Winton's deed seems to be spreading something I call a "positive virus," which has affected most of the rescued children. Many of them feel that they must somehow repay for having been rescued by helping others. Several have adopted or fostered orphans. Others work as volunteers in hospitals, or for charitable organizations. My greatest pleasure is to learn that the "virus" has also affected children, our young generation, in many countries. Many of them have decided to act positively to try to make our world a better place. That is our greatest reward and it fills me with optimism and conviction that spreading Winton´s message is a worthy endeavor. We present you in the supplementary material with the initiative of the Congressman Tom Lantos who is one of the leading forces to honor Sir Nicholas

Winton in the U.S. We believe it will be also interesting to get acquainted with the life story of Congressman Tom Lantos, who was also as child rescued by Raoul Wallenberg in Hungary.

HOLOCAUST RESCUERS RECOGNIZED IN CONGRESS

On July 31, 2007, the Office of Congressman Tom Lantos conducted an open forum in the U.S. Congress to honor Raoul Wallenberg and Nicholas Winton, two men who saved the lives of thousands of European Jews before and during World War II. Mrs. Annette Lantos, wife of Congressman Tom Lantos, herself a Holocaust survivor saved by Wallenberg, moderated the event.

Raoul Wallenberg, a Swede, saved an estimated 100,000 Hungarian Jews over the course of the war, and subsequently perished in the Soviet prison system during the Cold War era.

Sir Nicholas Winton was a 29-year-old English stockbroker when he saved the lives of 669 Jewish and non-Jewish Czechoslovak children during the months before the outbreak of World War II. Mr. Winton recently celebrated his 98th birthday in his native England where he lives today.

The Forum included a 20-minute screening of the documentary *Nicholas Winton: The Power of Good,* which chronicles the story of Nicholas Winton saving the 669 Czechoslovak children and highlights the lives some of them went on to live. It also featured a 7-minute clip from the television show *60 Minutes* about Mr. Wallenberg's rescue efforts that included Mrs. Lantos recounting her personal story and discussing Mr. Wallenberg's post-war fate.

Following the screenings, several guest speakers discussed their personal experiences with the two rescuers.

Mr. Peter Rafaeli, Honorary Consul General of the Czech Republic in Philadelphia, PA, spoke of Winton's extraordinary accomplishments achieved through Winton's personal philosophy that anything can be accomplished as long as it is not absolutely impossible.

Jaroslav Kurfürst, Deputy Ambassador of the Czech Republic, spoke of Winton's heroism and compassion toward humanity even though Winton does not consider himself a hero. Mr. Kurfurst attended the event on behalf of Czech Ambassador Petr Kolář who was unable to attend.

Two of the children saved by Winton, **Alice Masters** of Bethesda, MD, and **Dr. Benjamin Abeles** of New Jersey, shared their stories. Alice Masters, whose two sisters also were saved, pointed out that

Deputy Chief of Mission – Czech Embassy, Washington, DC and Peter A. Rafaeli speak on Capitol Hill on July 31, 2007

Panelists R. to L.: Jaroslav Kurfürst, Peter A. Rafaeli, Dr. Benjamin Abeles (Winton child), Alice Masters (Winton child), and Kayla Kaufman (saved by Raoul Wallenberg)

Mrs. Annette Lantos, wife of California Congressman Tom Lantos chairing the Wallenberg-Winton panel on Capitol Hill on July 31, 2007

The Power of Good contains footage of her mother putting her little sister on the transport and taking her off three times before she was finally able to pull herself away from her girls. The three sisters never saw their parents again.

Ms. Kayla Kaufman of New York, who was saved by Wallenberg, spoke about post-traumatic stress syndrome and her personal struggle with the memories of her family's escape.

Concurrent to the Wallenberg Forum, the House Committee on Foreign Affairs unanimously approved House Resolution No. 583 to honor Nicholas Winton and those who helped with his rescue effort. Resolution 583 will go to the House floor for debate when Congress reconvenes after the August recess.

HOUSE RESOLUTION NO. 583 STATES THAT:

"The House of Representatives commends Sir Nicholas Winton and those British and Czechoslovakian citizens who worked with him, for their remarkable persistence and selfless courage in saving the lives of 669 Czechoslovak Jewish children in the months before the outbreak of World War II, and urges men and women everywhere to recognize in Winton's remarkable humanitarian effort the difference that one devoted principled individual can make in changing and improving the lives of others."

ABOUT T.H. TOM LANTOS, MEMBER OF CONGRESS

Tom Lantos is serving his fourteenth term in the U.S. House of Representatives. He was first elected to Congress in November 1980. He won his seat by the lowest plurality of any Member of Congress elected that year: 46% to his opponent's 43%. Through excellent constituent service, careful attention to his district's needs, and hard work in the Bay Area and in Washington, Tom has been reelected repeatedly by large margins.

An American by choice, Tom (Thomas Peter) Lantos was born in Budapest, Hungary, on February 1, 1928. He was 16 years old when Nazi Germany occupied his native country. As a teenager, he was placed in a Hungarian fascist forced labor camp. He succeeded in escaping and was able to survive in a safe house in Budapest set up by Swedish humanitarian Raoul Wallenberg. His story is one of the individual accounts that forms the basis of Steven Spielberg's Academy Award-winning documentary about the Holocaust in Hungary, *The Last Days*. An article about Tom's background in World War II and the Spielberg film was published in the University of Washington alumni magazine. The San Francisco Examiner also published an article focusing on Tom's background.

In 1947, Tom was awarded an academic scholarship to study in the United States on the basis of an essay he wrote about U.S. President Franklin D. Roosevelt.

In August of that year, he arrived in New York City after a week-long boat trip to America on a converted World War II troop ship. His only possession was a precious Hungarian salami, which U.S. customs officials promptly confiscated when he arrived. Just a few weeks after he left Hungary, the Communist party seized control of the country.

Tom attended the University of Washington in Seattle, where he received a B.A. and M.A. in Economics. He moved to San Francisco in 1950 and began graduate studies at the University of California, Berkeley, where he later received his Ph.D. in Economics. In the fall of 1950 he started teaching economics at San Francisco State University.

In the summer of 1950, Tom Lantos married his childhood sweetheart, Annette Tillemann. Their first home was a tiny apartment in San Francisco. After a few years, they were able to purchase a modest home in San Bruno, and they later bought a home in Millbrae, where their two daughters attended public

schools, and where Tom served for several years as a member of the Millbrae School Board.

For three decades, Tom Lantos was a professor of economics, an international affairs analyst for public television, and an economic consultant to businesses. He also served in senior advisory roles to members of the United States Senate.

The Lantos family includes 17 grandchildren Tom and Annette Lantos are the parents of two daughters - Annette and Katrina. Annette is married to Timber Dick, an independent businessman in Colorado, and they are the parents of ten children.

The Lantos Family includes 17 grandchildren

Katrina is married to Richard N. Swett, former New Hampshire Congressman (1991-1995) and former U.S. Ambassador to Denmark (1998-2001). The Swetts are the parents of seven children.

In 2007, the Nicholas Winton Educational Project received the auspices of the Foreign Minister of the Czech Republic, H.E Karel Scharzenberg. It also has the full support of the Czech Ambassador to the U.S., H.E. Petr Kolář, who was the driving force in bringing the "Winton story" to the attention of Congressman Lantos and Mrs. Lantos.

CZECH EMBASSY HOLOCAUST EDUCATIONAL OUTREACH

Czech Embassy
Washington, DC
January 2008

Marking the United Nations International Day of Commemoration of the Victims of the Holocaust on January 27, the Embassy of the Czech Republic in Washington, DC, conducts an annual Holocaust Educational Outreach program to students between the ages of 12 and 18 in the United States. The Embassy launched this initiative in 2007 when more than 150 students from the Washington metropolitan area came to the Czech Consulate over a 4-day period to view the "Neighbors Who Disappeared" Exhibit. Marie Zahradnikova, the exhibit's curator from the Jewish Museum in Prague, presented the project which was produced by contemporary Czech school children who became curious about the fate of families who disappeared from their hometowns during the Nazi era. Ms. Zahradnikova's presentation to U.S. students included a historical overview of Jews in the Czech lands and the effects of World War II on the Czech Jewish population. After viewing the exhibit for themselves, students assumed the identity of one of the disappeared neighbors, then wrote and presented their stories to classmates.

Czech Ambassador Petr Kolář greets Alice Masters (Winton child) at the Library of Congress

In 2008, the Embassy of the Czech Republic, with the support of the Israeli and British Embassies, continues the Holocaust Educational Outreach program using the story of Nicholas Winton, a young Briton who helped save the lives of 669 Czechoslovak Jewish and non-Jewish children during the run-up to WWII. The in-school initiative includes screening

Peter Rafaeli introducing the film Nicholas Winton: The Power of Good at the Library of Congress, January 2008

the documentary, *Nicholas Winton: The Power of Good*, followed by a discussion and presentation by Holocaust educator Dr. Miriam Klein Kassenhoff and questions and answers with Alice Masters, one of the children saved by Winton. Film screenings and discussion will also take place at the Library of Congress and at the Magen-David Sephardic Congregation in Rockville, MD.

The Attorney General of the United States takes an interest in the Nicholas Winton story

Phil Kasik, former AFoCR president greets Alice Masters
with Jeff Turner, Esq. and Peter Rafaeli in the background

American Friends of the Czech Republic (AFoCR) has been pivotal in bringing the Winton story to the American public. Their promotional efforts led to a special letter of recognition from President Bush to Nicholas Winton in July 2006, the passage of House Resolution 583 by the U.S. House of Representatives honoring Sir Winton for his heroic actions, and publication of the educational book

Dr. Nora Jurkovičová, from the
Czech Embassy with Alice Masters

Nicholas Winton's Lottery of Life by Matej Mináč and translated from the Czech by AFoCR president Peter Rafaeli. AFoCR is currently distributing 17,000 free copies of the book to educational institutions nationwide upon request. In October 2007, Mr. Rafaeli and Ambassador Petr Kolář traveled to Prague to attend a week-long series of events that honored Sir Winton that included a visit with Czech President Vaclav Klaus, a reception at the residence of Ambassador Richard Graber, recognition at Vaclav Havel's Forum 2000, and a Prague gala attended by more than 3,000 guests, including 2,700 school children.

For more information on the Holocaust Educational Outreach program conducted by the Embassy of the Czech Republic in Washington, DC, please call JoAnn M. Cooper at (202) 274-9126.

The Right Rev. John Bryson Chane, D.D., Episcopalian Bishop of Washington greets Alice Masters as British Ambassador looks on

L to R: H.E. Sir Nigel Sheinwald, British Ambassador to the U.S., Lady Sheinwald, H.E. PhDr. Petr Kolář, Czech Ambassador to the U.S., Mrs. Alice Masters, Mrs. Kolářová, H.E. Sallai Meridor, Israeli Ambassador to the U. S., and Mrs. Meridor

Presentation of gifts by American Friends of the Czech Republic president Peter Rafaeli to the British, Czech and Israeli Ambassadors

At the conclusion of the Czech Embassy's Holocaust Outreach at a suburban Washington school, this boy was so touched by the film and presentation that he called his mother to immediately bring a bouquet of flowers for Mrs. Alice Masters

**Printed in the USA by and with the support
of Thomson-Shore, Inc., Dexter, MI**